A SHIJO POET AT THE COURT OF KING SONJO

A Shijo Poet at the Court of King Sonjo: The Pine River Songs is a translation of *Songgang kasa*, Chong Ch'ol's (1536-1593) famous collection of Korean songs. The translations are by Kevin O'Rourke, one of the foremost translators of Korean literature into English in the world today. Professor O'Rourke includes in the volume a biographical sketch of the Choson dynasty poet-official and a critical analysis of his work. These essays provide a fascinating background to the life and work of this enigmatic man.

Royal Inspector, governor of a province, personal secretary to the king, second prime minister, general of the army - these are some of the positions held by Chong Ch'ol during a career that was punctuated by periods of voluntary retirement, dismissal and exile. He was by nature a brilliant but rather stubborn man. Loved by his friends, hated by his enemies, his life was marked by continuous controversy. Korean commentators traditionally regard Chong Ch'ol as the greatest exponent of the essay-poem genre called kasa– his kasa were immensely popular in his own lifetime - and they consistently place him among the great shijo poets. Readers of *A Shijo Poet at the Court of King Sonjo: The Pine River Songs* will be struck by the literary quality of the shijo, which are without peer in the history of the genre, and by the urbanity and cultivation of the kasa poems. These poems come alive for the first time in English versions that stand on their own as English poems.

Kevin O'Rourke is professor of English at Kyunghee University in Seoul. An Irish priest (Columban Fathers), he has lived in Korea since 1964. The first foreigner to receive a PhD in Korean literature (Yonsei University 1982), he has published many translations of classical and contemporary texts and also many critical essays on themes related to Korean literature. For many years Kevin O'Rourke's poetry column in the Korea Herald, *A Poem for Breakfast*, has provided expatriates with a real insight into the riches of Korean literature and culture.

A SHIJO POET AT THE COURT OF KING SONJO

The Pine River Songs

KEVIN O'ROURKE

LONDON AND NEW YORK

This translation by Kevin O'Rourke first published in 2004 by Kegan Paul.

This edition first published in 2009 by
Routledge
2 Park Square, Milton Park, Abingdon, Oxfordshire OX14 4RN

Simultaneously published in the USA and Canada
by Routledge
711 Third Avenue, New York, NY 10017

First issued in paperback 2016

Routledge is an imprint of the Taylor & Francis Group, an informa business

© Kegan Paul 2004

All rights reserved. No part of this book may be reprinted or reproduced or utilised in any form or by any electronic, mechanical, or other means, now known or hereafter invented, including photocopying and recording, or in any information storage or retrieval system, without permission in writing from the publishers.

British Library Cataloguing in Publication Data
A catalogue record for this book is available from the British Library

ISBN 13: 978-1-138-98183-6 (pbk)
ISBN 13: 978-0-7103-0981-5 (hbk)

Publisher's Note
The publisher has gone to great lengths to ensure the quality of this reprint but points out that some imperfections in the original copies may be apparent. The publisher has made every effort to contact original copyright holders and would welcome correspondence from those they have been unable to trace.

For Anne and Joe

Acknowledgments

Sincere thanks are due to Pak Kidawk, Han Kyongshim and Katherine Lee for unstinting help in preparing the manuscript.

Acknowledgment is made of the support of the Korean Literature Translation Institute in making and publishing these translations.

Poems in this collection have previously appeared in Tilting the Jar, Spilling the Moon (Dedalus 1993), The Book of Korean Shijo (Harvard 2002), Korea Herald, Korea Times, Korea Journal, and Koreana.

Contents

Chong Ch'ol: Biographical Sketch	1
Chong Ch'ol: Critical Essay	9
Untitled *Shijo*	
People of Kangwon Province	31
I race through Kwanghwamun	31
On Pongnaesan where my true love lives	32
Stock from boiled bitter greens	32
When did Liu Ling live	32
Listen here	33
Whether I eat wheat bran or rice chaff	33
Ten years I followed you	34
If you truly hoped to achieve something	34
I say it once again	34
Human life lasts a hundred years	35
If I lifted my wings	35
I wish to dismember my body	35
I'll cut out my heart	36
The rise and fall of nations are myriad	36
When Shin Kunmang was a fifth rank official	36
When the South Pole Star	37
That zelkova planted on the terrace	37
Crane, flying high	37
When I strike the great string of the komun'go	38
When my long feathers molt	38
Now that I'm keeper of the state guesthouse	39
Now that I'm keeper of the state guesthouse	39
Now that I'm keeper of the state guesthouse	39
When I think of King Chang Sha's tutor	40
I'm aware that I'm not	40

The tree is diseased	40
Yesterday I heard that Master Song	41
After a ten-year interval I see again	41
What happens if you pull down	41
Holding back a horse laugh	42
No moaning, please	42
We'll strain sour wine and drink	42
A tall Shilla pagoda	43
A sudden shower	43
Where has the crane gone	43
I'll wash and rewash	44
Somewhere on Namsan Mountain	44
My old loves are still my loves	44
I'm fifty now, no longer young	45
My carelessness	45
Shall I put my worries aside	45
Don't waken babies from sweet sleep	46
Forty thousand boxes of bright jewels	46
Somehow or other	46
As I move the goosefoot forward	47
The falling paulownia leaves	47
I've been gone such a very long time	47
Clouds shrouded	48
When our droopy-eared horse	48
Take all the misfortunes	48
Snow falling in the pine forest	49
A shadow is reflected in the water	49
The lad has gone to dig fernbrake	49
Were I brilliant	50
Butterflies hover in pairs where flowers blossom thick	50
Pearly raindrops on green hills	50
Sleep bound birds fly home	51
The evening sun slants low	51
Two stone Buddhas, naked and fasting	51
Husband dead	52
Where is that boat going	52
Why does that pine tree stand	52
White gull	53
When did the leaves come out	53
Genuine jade, they said	53
Fishermen of the Chu River	54
I promised to return to rivers and lakes	54
When the paulownia leaves fell	54

Hunmin ka (Instructing the People)
  Father's Honor; Mother's Affection   55
  King and Subject   55
  Respect between Brothers   55
  Filial Piety   56
  Grace between Spouses   56
  Distinction between the Sexes   56
  Educating Children   57
  Etiquette among Villagers   57
  Order between Old and Young   57
  Trust between Friends   58
  Family Support in Poverty and Calamity   58
  Mutual Help in Marriage and Death   58
  Farm the Land and Cultivate Silkworms Assiduously   59
  Do Not Steal   59
  No Gambling, No Litigation   59
  Don't Let an Old timer Carry a Burden on the Road   60

Sasol shijo or *kasa*
Changjinju sa (An Inducement to Imbibe)   61

Kasa
Samiin kok (Love Song)   62
Sokmiin kok (Love Song Continued)   67
Kwandong pyolgok (Song of the East Coast)   71
Songsan pyolgok (Song of Mount Star)   82

Bibliography   89

Index of First Lines   91

Chong Ch'ol: Biographical Sketch

Chong Ch'ol (1536-1593) was the youngest of six children in a not very prominent noble family that advanced itself through marriage into the royal family. Chong Ch'ol's elder sister was married to Injong; his second sister was married to Prince Kyerim. A regular visitor to the palace as a boy, he was particularly friendly with the future king Myongjong.

In 1545, Injong came to the throne. Dead within eight months, he was succeeded by his half-brother, Myongjong, who was just a boy at the time. Myongjong's accession was followed by the great Ulsa purge of 1545. Orchestrated by Yun Wonhyong, younger brother of Myongjong's mother, Queen Munjong, the Ulsa purge was an attempt to aggrandize power. Prince Kyerim, who belonged to Injong's side of the family, the opposition in the struggle for power, was promptly executed, and his wife's family, Chong Ch'ol's family, was swept into the ensuing vortex: Chong Ch'ol's father was sent into exile and his eldest brother died on his way into exile, a victim of the severe torture he had endured. Chong Ch'ol, only ten years old at the time, followed his father into exile, first to Kwanbuk, subsequently to Chongbyong, and finally to Yonil, where he remained until Myongjong lifted the decree of exile in 1551.

The Chong family now moved to Ch'angp'yong near Tamyang in Cholla Province. Chong Ch'ol lived in Ch'angp'yong until he passed the civil service examination. Kim Yunjae, his master, had retired from the bureaucracy at the time of the Ulsa purge. Returning to Tamyang, he had set up a sort of school-salon, which had become the cultural center of the area. Chong Ch'ol studied poetry under Im Okryong (1496-1568) and Ki Taesung (1527-1572); he also received instruction from Song Sun (1493-1583) and Kim Inhu (1519-1560), prominent literati of the period, and he was on friendly terms with the *hanshi* poets Paek Kwanghun and Ch'oe Kyongch'ang, and such prominent men of letters as Yi T'oegye, Yi

Yulgok, Song Hon and Song Ikp'il. Im Okryong, magistrate of Tamyang, became Chong Ch'ol's poetry teacher in 1558. An important hanshi poet (Korean poet writing Chinese verse), Im was skilled in Tang poetry, notably Li Bai style, at a time when the Song tradition was in the ascendancy. He was sixty-three years old; Chong Ch'ol was twenty-three. The master obviously had political ambitions that had not been realized. "Cold Moon on Autumn Mountain" expresses his feelings:

> The autumn mountain throws up a cold moon;
> it hangs through the night on the paulownia in the yard.
> I've waited long for the noble phoenix;
> it will hardly come in my lifetime now

Chong Ch'ol's reply is filled with a graciousness surprising in such a young man:

> The master's poems have the phoenix heart;
> the moon hangs in the paulownia branches.
> White hair fills the autumn moon;
> the worn face is that of a hero.

In 1561, Chong Ch'ol passed the civil service examination at the *chinsa* level, the equivalent of a modern undergraduate degree. In 1562, he took first place in the *shimungwa* (Chinese classics examination) and began his public career as an arbitrator in the Office of the Inspector General. His childhood friend, Myongjong, welcomed him to court. Indeed Myongjong saw to it personally that he got the position in the office of the Inspector General. This should have been a happy period for the young bureaucrat, but unfortunately, Myongjong's cousin, Prince Kyongyang, in a ploy to get control of his wife's family property, murdered his wife's brother. Myongjong suggested lenience, but Chong Ch'ol insisted on the rigor of the law. Father and son were executed. Chong Ch'ol's relationship with the king never recovered. While Myongjong remained king, advancement for Chong Ch'ol in the bureaucracy was effectively blocked; he circled in a series of low-level posts, an easy target for his enemies.

Sonjo's accession to the throne in 1567 marked a new beginning for Ch'ong Chol's official career. Intent on bringing into the government all the young men of talent he could muster, Sonjo granted his special favor to Chong Ch'ol and to Yi Yulgok (1536-1584), who was one of Korea's greatest Confucian scholars.

The next few years were very active in the young official's life. He appears to have been very outspoken in court, unwavering in his support of righteousness. In 1570, his father died, and mourning etiquette demanded that he withdraw from court activities. Two years of formal graveside mourning ensued before he returned to the bureaucracy. In 1573, his mother died, entailing a further two years of formal mourning. He returned to court in 1575.

Meanwhile, the great Easterner-Westerner factional battles had begun. Ch'ong Ch'ol's political fortunes ebbed and flowed with the oscillations of the battle between the rival groups. Initially, Kim Hyowon (1532-1590) and Shim Uigyom (1535-1587) were at the center of the controversy, but eventually they both faded into obscurity. The row began in 1575 over the appointment of the secretary in the Ministry of Appointments. This was not a ranking post, but it was a position that wielded significant power. The incumbent (Kim Hyowon) had the right to nominate his successor. Shim Uigyom, however, had opposed Kim's appointment to the post, so Kim now opposed the appointment of Shim's brother as his successor. The *sarim* (Confucian scholars) in the government took sides. Kim lived in east Seoul; his supporters were known as the Easterners (Tongin). Shim lived in west Seoul; his supporters were called the Westerners (Soin). The Easterners were radical reformers; the Westerners were doves. The Easterners divided into Southerners (Namin) and Northerners (Pugin); the Westerners divided into Noron and Soron. The Easterners followed the teachings of Yi T'oegye, and the Westerners followed the teachings of Yi Yulgok.

There had been a rebellion in Hwanghae Province. Kim Hyowon's group sought to impeach Pak Sun (1523-1589) for his handling of the affair. Chong Ch'ol, a mere four months back in court at the time, vehemently opposed the move and tried to get Yulgok to restrain Kim Hyowon's Easterners. Disappointed with Yulgok's efforts and knowing that Sonjo was not going to do anything about the situation, he retired to the country despite Sonjo's efforts to dissuade him. He spent the next three years in the country, concentrating on what a *yangban* (nobleman) considered the finer things in life: study, poetry composition, music and wine. It was probably during this period that he wrote the *kasa* "Songsan pyolgok", which weighs the advantages of a life in harmony with nature against the glories to be attained in public life. It would seem certain that he still entertained political ambitions.

Factional rivalry ultimately was about power; Chong Ch'ol was at the heart of the battle.

In 1578, Chong Ch'ol returned to the court. During the next year he held ten different posts, testimony to the insecurity of his position. Yulgok, also fresh out of retirement, was anxious for peace between the rival factions. However, because he felt he had failed earlier in the role of peacemaker, he decided to take himself out of the equation and to cede responsibility to Chong Ch'ol. Instead of appease ment, however, factional rivalry gained in intensity.

Battle lines were drawn again when Yi Su, county chief of Chindo Island, was accused of giving a bribe of rice to the Yun brothers, who were ranking members of the Westerner faction. The charge was disputed, but the Easterners made a big issue out of it. Chong Ch'ol was censured for his support of the Yuns and he retired to Koyang, outside Seoul. In a memorial to the throne, Yulgok vouched for Chong Ch'ol's integrity and thus became a target himself for Easterner attack. The Easterners, now firmly in power, continued to vilify the Westerners. Chong Ch'ol returned to Ch'angp'yong.

In 1580, Chong Ch'ol was appointed Governor of Kangwon Province. He had refused a number of appointments offered after the Yi Su bribery scandal, but the governorship was an appointment he felt he had to accept for reasons of family prestige. "Kwandong pyolgok", the "Hunmin ka" *shijo* series and a large number of *hanshi* were written at this time.

In 1581, Chong Ch'ol was appointed Director of the National Academy. Denounced for his uncompromising attitude, he returned to Ch'angp'yong. In 1582, he became First Royal Secretary and Second Minister of Rites. He was appointed Minister of Rites in 1583, and Inspector General in 1584. These were splendid years for Chong Ch'ol. Despite constant vilification by the Easterners, he managed to retain a special place in the affections of Sonjo and to advance his official career continuously. In 1585, however, criticism of his drinking habits forced him to retire to the country again. The next four years marked a severe downturn in his political fortunes. They were years of great personal trial, his longest period out of office. Friends interceded on his behalf. So Ik (1542-1587) and Cho Hon (1544-1592) both sent memorials to the king pleading Chong Ch'ol's cause, but such was the power of the Easterners in the court that Sonjo did not give Chong Ch'ol's friends a hearing. Eventually there was no one left to plead for him. Beset by feelings of rejection and political alienation, he wrote the two famous "love of the king" *kasa*, "Samiin kok" and "Sokmiin kok." The official literary view is that these two masterpieces show the poet-official transcending his personal problems in his literary works. This seems an oversimplification of a complex emotional situation.

Chong Yorip's attempt to take power (The Kich'uk Affair) in 1589 provided the occasion for Chong Ch'ol's return to public office. Yi Yulgok had introduced Chong Yorip, a Westerner and a young man of exceptional promise, to the court. However, after Yulgok's death, Chong Yorip changed allegiance to the Easterner side when he saw that power rested firmly in the hands of the Easterner group and proceeded to excoriate his old teacher, Yulgok, an offence that his former Westerner colleagues were not going to forgive readily. The young man's deportment incurred the king's displeasure and he was sent to the country where the seeds of his rebellion were supposedly planted. In the event, there is some doubt as to whether there was a rebellion at all. The Easterners felt that Chong Ch'ol fabricated the entire affair. At any rate, Chong Ch'ol, who was living at the time in Koyang, outside Seoul, rushed to the king with a plan to deal with the enemies of the state. Sonjo, greatly impressed, restored his old friend to high office. In 1589, he appointed him Minister of the Right, and in 1590, Minister of the Left, both appointments of prime minister rank.

Chong Ch'ol's promotion in the government proved a mixed blessing. Against a background of increasing rancor and viciousness among the factions, he used his political position in prosecuting the case against the rebels to destroy some of the leading Easterners. Yi Pal (1544-1589), a close friend of Chong Yorip and a lifelong enemy of Chong Ch'ol, was cruelly tortured. He paid the ultimate price along with his aged mother and eight year old son. The Yi Pal - Chong Ch'ol enmity story went back to when they were both young men. Chong Ch'ol, an onlooker at a *paduk* game, offered some unsolicited and unwelcome advice, to which Yi Pal retorted, "How dare the son of a traitor give advice here!" Then he crowned the insult with a yank on Chong Ch'ol's beard! Petty wrangling indeed, but seemingly time had not assuaged the affront. At least, the Easterners felt that Chong Ch'ol was now taking his revenge. Ch'oe Yonggyong (1529-1590), another close friend of Yi Pal, was also implicated in the Chong Yorip plot. He was an upright man who refused office repeatedly because of his horror of factional politics. He died under interrogation. Chong Ch'ol made many enemies in his ruthless prosecution of the crown's case.

In 1591, Chong Ch'ol made another political mistake when he proposed Kwanghaegun as Crown Prince, thus incurring the wrath of the king who favored Prince Shinsong. Subsequently, he was accused of plotting against Prince Shinsong and the prince's mother, a favorite of Sonjo. Censured by the Chief State Councilor, Yi Sanhae, leader of the Easterners, he was dismissed from his post and sent into exile. The extraordinary thing about this affair was that Kwanghaegun was the candidate of the Easterners. Chong Ch'ol would not have supported him unless he thought it was in the national interest. Presumably Yi Sanhae duped him into thinking this and then proceeded to censor him. The affair can be seen as one chapter in the book of Easterner revenge. For Chong Ch'ol, it was the beginning of another difficult, soul-searching period, but by this time he had become fatalistic in his attitude.

The Hideyoshi Wars broke out in 1592, and the king fled to P'yongyang. Chong Ch'ol was recalled from exile, ostensibly in consideration of his record of loyalty, but in reality because he was sorely needed by the king. He went directly to P'yongyang in order to escort the king to Uiju. Afterwards he came south to involve himself in military affairs with a view to retaking Seoul. Subsequently he went to Ming China as a member of the war delegation. The court returned to Seoul in 1593.

In 1594, Chong Ch'ol was censured once again by the Easterners, who maintained he had failed in his mission to the Ming court. It would appear the delegation to Beijing announced prematurely that the war was coming to an end. Ming, already gravely weakened internally, wanted to withdraw their forces quickly. Once again Chong Ch'ol was scapegoated by his enemies. He retired to Kanghwa Island where he died in pain and poverty, a sad end to an exciting if troubled life.

What sort of man was Chong Ch'ol? The commentators point to his solid grounding in Confucianism, and they name Im Okryong and Kim Inhu as Confucian masters who were particularly influential in the formation of the young man's character. They do not go into specifics but are content to enumerate the standard Confucian virtues: loyalty, filial piety, devotion to justice, and fidelity to the practices of ritual etiquette. They illustrate these virtues from episodes in Chong Ch'ol's life and from individual poems. The years he spent in mourning his parents, for example, demonstrate his filial piety and his observance of ritual etiquette; his refusal to yield to Myongjong's plea of lenience for an erring cousin shows his dedication to the principles of justice; the love of the king poems show his great loyalty. The commentators do not dwell on his reasons for repeatedly refusing offers of posts in the government, or on the moral implications of his drinking habits when he was a magistrate. They do not account satisfactorily either for the attraction of his personality, or for his bad relationships with so many fellow bureaucrats.

The commentators also point to the importance of Taoism in Chong Ch'ol's formation, and they name his friend Kim Songwon, the hermit hero of "Songsan pyolgok, as an important mentor in his emerging philosophy of life. Taoism is used to explain the sense of fatalistic inevitability with which he greeted the various ups and downs of his career. His abiding interest in the world of the Immortals is understood in terms of his pursuit of an ideal world. The nihilism of Taoism, with its emphasis on the transitory nature of human life and the ephemerality of human glory, is used to explain his drinking habits. The pleasures of wine are presented as a Taoist antidote to the pain of life.

The methodology of tracing Confucian and Taoist characteristics to episodes in Chong Ch'ol's life and illustrating these characteristics by individual poems is not very convincing. Materials can always be manipulated to suit one's purposes. What is certain from a study of the available records is that Chong Ch'ol was a man of striking physical appearance, that he had a large circle of friends, among whom were numbered many of the outstanding men of the age, and an equally large circle of enemies, among whom were also numbered many outstanding men. His friends, who were mostly Westerners, said he was upright, loyal, dedicated and filial. What negative criticism they made was couched in terms of stubborn intransigence and over-devotion to duty. His enemies, Easterners for the most part, said he was greedy and avaricious. Snake and wolf were their favorite epithets. Praise and blame here appear to be the vocabulary of factional allegiance. Neutral commentators said he was a loyal, upright official but inclined to be narrow minded and intolerant. It would appear from all this that there was something of the Jekyll and Hyde in Chong Ch'ol's personality. When he drank socially and his writing brush began to fly, he had the mien of an Immortal and all social differences disappeared, which meant in effect that he was a very amiable drinking companion. When he drank on the job, however, he spoke stridently. He was mean and unforgiving; and he tore to shreds anyone who opposed him. Hangover symptoms presumably. His ruthless prosecution of the Chong Yorip affair raises major character questions. His conduct of the case was blatantly cruel.

Finally, his alcohol problems cannot be adequately dealt with under the heading of Taoist solace in an ephemeral world. Alcohol was a way of life for *p'ungnyu* men and Chong Ch'ol was undoubtedly a *p'ungnyu* man. Ch'oe Ch'iwon of Shilla defined *p'ungnyu* as a fine amalgam of Buddhism, Taoism and Confucianism. Ch'oe Namson claimed that the old Korean term *pu-ru,* meaning the light of heaven, was matched to the Chinese characters *p'ung* and *ryu* (wind and flow). *P'ungnyu* then was the light of heaven in a man's inner being. The practice of *p'ungnyu,* however, always had strong overtones of music, poetry, wine, and *kisaeng.* Whether *p'ungnyu* for Chong Ch'ol meant the light of heaven in the heart, or a convivial night of wine, poetry and music in the company of *kisaeng* is difficult to say. Perhaps it meant both. This would account for some of the ambivalence in the man.

Chong Ch'ol: Critical Essay

Cho Kyuik begins his study of the *kagok-ch'angsa* (literally *kagok*-song-lyric, his preferred term for the genre more commonly called *shijo*) by pointing out that Korea has two poetry traditions: the *hanshi* tradition (poems in Chinese following the rules of Chinese prosody), which is a poetry to be read and contemplated; and the vernacular tradition (*hyangga*, Koryo *kayo, kasa* and what today we call *shijo*), which is a poetry to be sung and heard. The common denominator across the vernacular songs, he tells us, is the *kasa*, literally music words. *Kasa* includes under its umbrella all vernacular songs. The songs we call *shijo* today – *shijo* as a term referring to a literary text is a twentieth century coinage - are a subdivision of *kasa*. Originally sung to the *kagok-ch'ang*, the accompaniment was complex, featuring five sung sections and two musical interludes, and requiring the services of a considerable ensemble. The *shijo-ch'ang*, a much simpler musical accompaniment, featuring three sung sections, whose rhythms could be beaten out on a drum or, if needs be, on the thigh of the singer, was not developed until the middle of the 19th century. Scholars are not sure exactly when.[1] The songs we call *kasa* today, are a specific genre that developed either at the end of Koryo or at the beginning of Choson. Scholars hardly agree on anything about the genre except that it is a four-*umbo* (breath-group) structure. They are not even agreed on whether it is prose or poetry. Some see *kasa* primarily as prose or as an essay in verse-song form; others see *kasa* as song; still others divide the genre into *kasa* song and *kasa* essay; Cho Tongil posits a new genre, neither drama,

---

[1] Cho Kyuik, *Kagokch'angsaui kungmunhakchok ponjil* (The essence of the *kagok-ch'ang* song lyric in the Korean literature tradition) (Seoul: Chimmundang, 1994), pp. 19-77.

lyric, nor epic, a genre whose primary focus is didactic.[2]

Since Chinese was the language of literature throughout the Choson dynasty, Chong Ch'ol's primary literary vehicle was *hanshi*. He is credited with 763 *hanshi* and four *pu* (odes in Chinese characters). However, like many prominent poet-officials at the time, he also liked to compose in the vernacular. He is credited with four or five *kasa*, depending on whether "Changjinjusa" (An Invitation to Imbibe) is treated as a *kasa* or as a *sasol shijo*; and some 107 *shijo*, of which seventeen are of very doubtful ascription, and others more or less doubtful, leaving about eighty or ninety that are accepted by the commentators. These vernacular poems are collected in *Songgang kasa* (Pine River was Chong Ch'ol's penname). *A Shijo Poet in the Court of King Sonjo* is a translation of *Songgang kasa*.

Educated in the Confucian classics, Chong Ch'ol's earliest poetry training was in Chinese poetry. It seems reasonable therefore to conclude that the *hanshi* represent the poet's more serious literary side, whereas the *shijo* and *kasa* represent the poet in moments of leisure or at least in less formal literary mode. After all, the literati continued to treat the vernacular as *onmun* (vulgar language) until the end of the nineteenth century when nationalist considerations endowed the native language with new meaning and energy. This assessment, however, must not be pushed too far. The literary quality of many of the *shijo* is self-evident and the *kasa* are the work of an urbane, cultivated poet. Korean commentators traditionally revere Chong Ch'ol as the greatest exponent of the *kasa* genre – his *kasa* were immensely popular in his own lifetime - and they consistently place him among the master *shijo* poets. So, even if the *hanshi* far outstrip the vernacular poems in terms of volume and Choson dynasty prestige, the vernacular poems have carved their own lasting niche in terms of literary quality and creative genius. Today, in Korea, no one speaks of Chong Ch'ol's Chinese poems; he is remembered as a master vernacular poet.

Chong Ch'ol's poetry teachers, Im Okryong (1496-1568) and Ki Taesung (1527-1572), favored a return to the romantic, confessional tradition of Tang poetry in preference to the Song tradition, with its emphasis on structure, form, and classical allusion, which had been in the ascendancy in the first part of Choson. Ki Taesung explained

---

[2] For a discussion of the various theories, see So Wonpyon, *Han'guk kasaui munhakchok yon'gu* (A literary study of Korean kasa) (Seoul: Hyongsol ch'ulp'ansa, 1995), pp.33-38; and Cho Tongil, "Kasaui changnu kyujong" (Defining the kasa genre), Omunhak 21 ho (1969), p. 85.

the world in terms of *chong* (emotion) and *ki* (energy).[3] Poetry, he says, has to do with *chong*. A poem begins with an external object and then moves to the heart. The objective of the poem is to elicit *hung*, that inner excitement associated with *Zen* penetration of essences, which Korean poets consider to be the heart of the poetry experience. Master and student illustrate the point. Ki Taesung writes:

> In the front yard wildflower fragrance
>   balances on the breeze.
> It's like a dream; I waken from wine
>   drunk early in the day.
> Flowers flutter deep in the garden;
>   spring days are long.
> Over the bead curtain I see bees
>   and butterflies dizzily at play.

Chong Ch'ol's answering poem, "Duck Asleep on the Sand" shows the student already outstripping the master:

> The wind gets up;
>   there's a gentle fluttering of wings.
> Colored plumage shimmers
>   even more beautifully in the sun.
>   Dive complete,
>   the duck leaves the water;
>   the sand is so warm,
>   he sinks into sleep.

Ki Taesung's poem begins with the scene in the yard, which he describes by focusing on flower fragrance. This is his cue to move to the heart, to his feelings of being in a dream paradise, which generate the *hung* mood. The poem, however, is filled with conventional images from the Chinese tradition. Spring flower fragrance, the wine that brings heightened awareness, the joy of spring as reflected in the joy of the smallest insects, and the implied ephemeral nature of existence -- all these are conventional. Fragrance "balancing" on the breeze is the only creative image in the poem.

---

[3] Pak Yongju, *Chong Ch'ol P'yongjon* (A Critical Biography of Chong Ch'ol), (Seoul: Chungang M&B), 1999, p. 51

Chong Ch'ol's poem is much more accomplished. He observes the duck very closely, catching the colors of spring, the duck's languid movements and the laziness of the spring mood. The duck comes out of the water and sinks into the warm sand - an elegant description of the poet's own feelings of *hung*. This is symbolist poetry three hundred years before the French invented the term, first-rate stuff and a useful yardstick against which to measure Chong Ch'ol's *shijo* and *kasa*.

Something quite extraordinary happened to Korean poetry at the beginning of the Choson dynasty. Simply stated, passion disappeared. Take, for example, the opening stanza of the Koryo *kayo* "Spring Pervades the Pavilion":

> I make a bed of bamboo leaves;
> I spread them on the ice.
> Though my love and I should freeze unto death,
>   slowly, slowly, pass this night
>   in love's enduring gentleness.

There is nothing like this in Choson poetry, not at least until Hwang Chini's famous mid-winter night *shijo*, which was written some two hundred years into the dynasty:

> I'll cut a piece from the waist
> of this interminable eleventh moon night,
> and wind it in coils beneath these bedcovers,
>   warm and fragrant as the spring breeze,
>   coil by coil
>   to unwind it the night my lover returns.

This is *kisaeng* poetry free from the constraints that circumscribed most *yangban* poetry. Chong Ch'ol has nothing comparable. In fact, a rare attempt to be sexually daring ends up in something rather coarse in the *shijo* that he built around a pun on a *kisaeng's* name, Chin'ok (Pure Jade), with whom he was on intimate terms.

> Genuine jade, they said;
> I thought it mere imitation.
> Now that I see it, I must admit, it is indeed pure jade.
> I have
> a fleshly awl and with it I will drill.

The redeeming wit of Chin'ok's purported reply, punning on

Chong Ch'ols name (pure ore) takes away a measure of Chong Ch'ol's crudeness:

> Metal I thought, yes,
> but metal of an inferior kind.
> Now I see it's metal of the purest mint.
> I have a bellows:
> I think I ought to melt that metal down.

Passion would not be tolerated in Choson. Yi T'oegye, a pillar of Choson dynasty Confucian orthodoxy, to whom the reforming Easterners looked for inspiration, frowned at such poems. He regarded them as a vulgar, corrupting influence, which ought to be kept out of the reach of children. In Eliot's terms, Choson society experienced a sort of dissociation of sensibility. Passion left Korean poetry and it did not begin to return until teachers like Ki Taesung in the sixteenth century advocated a return to the Tang tradition of *chong* and *ki*.

When passion left Korean poetry, the moral aspect became dominant; indeed, the need for a physical poetry disappeared. Yi Kyubo (1168-1241), the great Koryo poet, describes the experience of drinking tea in physical terms:

> With a pot of tea I try an experiment in taste;
> it's like frozen snow going down my throat.

He pinpoints the joy of *paduk*:

> The pleasure is in the clinking of the stones.

These images focus on the physical; taste and sound leap off the page with fresh immediacy. In the poetry of Choson, the physical is rare; the central emphasis is moral. Chong Pyong'uk tells us that Korean poets are never interested in the physically beautiful. When they look at a flower or a mountain they do not see something beautiful in physical terms, they see a symbol of a beautiful moral quality.[4] There is very little physical description in the *hanshi* of Yi Saek, Kil Chae, So Kojong or Kim Shisup, accomplished though these poets may be. Pinghodang's "Final Couplet", written early in the sixteenth century is so unusual, it startles:

---

[4] Chong Pyong'uk, *Han'guk kojonui chaeinshik*, (Seoul: Sasongshinso), 1979, pp. 339-348

> A jade ribbon hangs from the eaves;
> silver bells make circles where they drop.

Nam Sshi, a woman presumed also to have lived in the early part of the sixteenth century, wrote a couplet, "Song of the Snow" that is even more startling:

> Snow falling on the ground:
> silkworms munching mulberry leaves.
> Snow flying through the air:
> butterflies lighting gently on flowers.

Poets simply had not written in this mode since the end of Koryo. Invariably a poem began with an image and moved quickly to an inner landscape. Chong Ch'ol's "Duck Asleep on the Sand" does indeed give the physical feel of the object, but it would be unwarranted to conclude that this effect is representative of his oeuvre. Physical description is rare in Chong Ch'ol's poems. Certainly it appears in some of the *shijo* but not all that often, and there are descriptive passages in the *kasa*, "Kwandong pyolgok," for example, that also reveal a keen sense of observation, but the "moral" emphasis remains dominant. As for passion, the love *kasa* and love *shijo* are about as close as Chong Ch'ol gets. However, the traditional allegorical interpretation of these poems in terms of love of the king does not help in making a case for passion. The sentiments expressed in "Samiin kok", however, are at least dramatic and forceful. We glimpse the ardor of a woman scorned. This had been missing from Korean poetry for several hundred years.

As a body of work, Chong Ch'ol's vernacular poems are a mixed bag, ranging from the fine descriptive passages and Confucian moral sentiments of "Kwandong pyolgok" to the ardor of "Samiin kok", and from the exquisite satire of the political *shijo* poems, which are without precedent in the earlier history of the *shijo* genre, to the bland, didactic rhetoric of the "Hunmin ka" series. In general, the *shijo* show the *hanshi* technique of beginning with an observed object before moving to a moral comment. Many of the *shijo* support the idea of a poetry centered on *chong*, but very few of them are concerned with eliciting *hung*. Chong Ch'ol's *shijo* rarely engage beauty as theme. They are much more practical: they are about wine, politics, relationship with the king, and the vagaries of the human heart. Satire and humor are the primary tools. There are exceptions. The *shijo* describing the scene after the *paduk* game, for example, elicits *hung*. Some of the wine poems also elicit *hung*. However, such *shijo* are rare. The best of the *shijo* are on a par with the best of the *hanshi* but for different reasons: their strength is a striking versatility in the use of language - the startling phrase, the spare elegant expression, the density of meaning, the use of irony, qualities quite distinct from the more traditional felicities of the *hanshi*. Chong Ch'ol's *shijo* are a milestone in the development of Korean as poetic language.

> What happens if you pull down
> beams and supports?
> A host of opinions greet the leaning skeleton house.
> Carpenters
> with rulers and ink keep milling around.

This depiction of the confusion in the court at the time of Hideyoshi's invasion has the edge of the surgeon's scalpel. The speaker sees the state as a ramshackle house. The images are clear, precise, and incisive; beams and supports are qualified and their meanings extended by the use of the word skeleton with all its connotations, and the final image of carpenters running around with rulers and ink provides comedy and irony. Chong Ch'ol's political allegory poems are his finest achievement in the *shijo* genre. When he depicts the insecurity of a politician's life, the isolation and rejection that accompany loss of office are palpable:

> The tree is diseased;
> no one rests in its pavilion.
> When it stood tall and verdant, no one passed it by.
> But the leaves
> have fallen, the boughs are broken; not even birds
> perch there now.

Again the speaker observes an object and builds a symbolic response. The broken tree as a symbol of sterility is as old as poetry itself. Note that the tree is not described in any detail.

  Ch'ong Ch'ol's poem depicting the dangers inherent in
political over-exposure is not quite to the same standard, but still the irony inherent in the poem makes it stand out from the work of most of his contemporaries:

> Why does that pine tree stand
> so near the road?

I wish it stood a little back, perhaps in the
   hollow behind.
     Everyone
   geared with rope and axe will want to cut it down.

Anyone familiar with Korea's spitting culture will smile at Chong Ch'ol's assessment of the factional fighting and consequent corruption that characterized his political world:

   White gull,
   floating on the water,
   it was an accident my spit hit you on the back.
   White gull,
   don't be angry: I spat because the world is a
   dirty place.

The desire for integrity, for inner cleanliness, has always been the mark of the cultivated man. Whatever about the contradictions in his character, Chong Ch'ol's best poems are pervaded by a fine sense of humanity; he seems to frame them within a very personal context. Perhaps more than anywhere else, these finer human feelings can be discovered in poems that deal with the theme of transcendence. Indeed the finest *shijo* seem to deal with this theme, but then perhaps the finest poetry always does.

   A shadow is reflected in the water;
   a monk is crossing the bridge.
 Monk, stay a moment; let me ask you where
    you're going?
     Pointing his stick
   at the clouds, he passes without a backward glance.

Here we see contrasted the disparate experience of two people, a monk who presumably has penetrated the secret of transcendence and a speaker represented as indolent but willing to learn. The focus in the poem is on the speaker. He is the one who is brought face to face with truth; he is the one who achieves the insight. The ability to perceive the transcendent in others and the lack of it in oneself is one of the distinguishing marks of the good poet. Chong Ch'ol had this quality:

   A sudden shower
   splatters a lotus leaf,

>   but I cannot find the track of water.
>   I wish my heart
>   were like that leaf, that nothing ever stained it.

The sigh of relief the poet gives in the following poem when he finds himself free of the burden of office is almost audible. This, however, is in part a conventional response. The ranking bureaucrats who affirmed such noble sentiments invariably had aspirations to return to office:

>   Pearly raindrops on green hills,
>   how can you deceive me?
> Sedge rain cape and horsehair hat, how can you deceive me?
>   Two days ago
>   I took off my silk robes; now nothing soilable remains.

Wine was Chong Ch'ol's nemesis. In his writings he notes that most of the messes in his life were caused by over-indulgence. How awful, he exclaims, to waken in the morning with a terrible head and not be able to remember the insults one may have ladled out the previous night! Several *shijo* deal with wine associated problems. As a group they do not reach the heights achieved in the political allegories, but the best of them are very fine indeed and show the poet's basic method, focusing on a central image with a strong injection of irony, very often in the form of the poet laughing at himself:

>   The lad has gone to dig fernbrake;
>   the bamboo grove is empty.
> Who will pick up the pieces scattered across
>   the *paduk* board?
>   Reclined
> against a pine tree root, inebriate, I do not feel
>   the approach of day.

Paduk (Go in Japan), a game like chess, is very popular in Korea. The poet paints a picture of himself as a new day dawns: drunk as a coot after the party, but in harmony with his world, except perhaps for a little tongue-in-cheek, Oscar Wilde style *yangban* humor, expressed in terms of regret that the boy who looks after him is not around to tidy up the place. This is one of Chong Ch'ol's best poems. It is perhaps significant that it reads more like a quatrain than a *shijo*.

Some of the wine *shijo* are part of a series, with the speaker addressing a personified wine character and the wine character answering. The sheer whimsy of these poems gives them a special charm. The speaker declares:

> Ten years I followed you
> believing I'd be an achiever.
> But you say you hate me, that I've achieved nothing.
> Perhaps
> I should write on temperance as a token of farewell.

Wine answers:

> If you truly hoped to achieve something,
>   would you have cultivated me from the start?
> You always seemed pleased to see me; so I followed
>   you around.
>   Now you tell me
>   I'm bad: you'll have to give me up!

Finally, the speaker declares his dilemma:

> I say it once again:
> I cannot live without you.
> You let me forget the bad and the bitter.
> Can I now
> discard an old friend in favor of a new love?

Not part of the series but certainly in the same vein, the speaker laughs wryly at his dependence:

> I'm fifty now, no longer young.
>   Yet wherever I go, at the mere sight of wine,
> I break into a broad toothy grin. What's wrong with me?
>   Wine is an old, old
>   acquaintance: I cannot ever forget him.

Finally, perhaps Chong Ch'ol's most praised wine poem:

> Yesterday I heard that Master Song
>   from over the hill has new wine.
> I kicked the ox to its feet, threw on a saddlecloth
>   and rode up here.

> Boy,
> is your master home? Tell him Chong Ch'ol
> has come.

Critics traditionally have regarded this poem as epitomizing the *mot* (elegance) of the *sonbi* (scholar). This is a poem, they maintain, of quintessential *hung*. If you visualize the incongruity of a ranking bureaucrat perched on the back of an ox, going unannounced to another man's house and declaring that it's party time, you will get the idea. To a Western sensibility it's mostly cheek; to a Korean sensibility it's style!

Chong Ch'ol's *kasa* are of special interest because of the *kasa* concept they enshrine. Western sensibility does not have a concept of an essay poem. Comparisons have been made with the pastoral tradition in England, but such comparisons do not stand up to scrutiny. English poetry, in fact, has nothing like the *kasa*. Korean *yangban* poets saw themselves in terms of harmony with a cleansing natural world; their *kasa* were songs, Choson's answer to the poetry challenge of Koryo. Instead of the passionate, unbridled emotion of Koryo *kayo*, *yangban kasa* presented an urbane, descriptive, essay-style poetry, which stuck to good Confucian doctrinal lines. *Kasa* advocated loyalty and fidelity, affirmed the primacy of self-cultivation, promoted harmony with nature, and controlled all excess of feeling. Only in its later development did the genre expand to include problems from the everyday lives of the people. The result was a safe, controlled poetry discourse. The essay or poem debate has been partially fuelled by the fact that *kasa* were recorded in continuous prose format. It should be pointed out that in many of the anthologies *shijo* were also recorded in continuous prose format. Whether *kasa* or *shijo*, the Korean poet's understanding of the poetry line is quite different from that of an English poet. For a Korean poet, the line tends to be arbitrary. This is inevitable in a poetry culture that does not employ meter, rhyme, assonance or dissonance and where position in the line is not of semantic significance. The breath unit, *umbo*, is the dominant consideration in Korean prosody.

There are two theories about when Chong Ch'ol wrote "Songsan pyolgok". One theory says he wrote it in 1560 as an immature young man of twenty-five. The second theory centers on the "washing the ears" phrase, which it interprets not just as a classical reference to the Chinese retainer who refused the offer of a kingdom, but as a reference to something Sonjo said to Yulgok when the latter asked for permission to retire from court in 1575. The incident left a bad taste because Sonjo's words seemed to imply that Yulgok was washing his hands of public affairs, taking the easy way out. Sonjo did not try to prevent Yulgok from going, nor did he withdraw his statement. Bad feeling continued through 1577 when Chong Ch'ol is surmised to have written the poem.

Songsan (Mount Star) is in Ch'angp'yong in Cholla Province. The poem celebrates the aesthetic life of Kim Songwon through the four seasons on Mount Star. Kim Songwon and Chong Ch'ol were particularly close friends although they were separated by an age gap of eleven years. They had studied together and Chong Ch'ol's wife was related to Kim.

"Songsan pyolgok" has a threefold structure: an introduction featuring the scene and introducing the hermit, the main body of the poem, which presents the delights of the place through the four seasons, and a conclusion, which is a meditation on history and on the current times. The introductory section has two parts. In the first part (lines 1-6), a wayfarer poses a question: Why does the master remain here in seclusion? The second part (lines 6-15) describes the scene around the house and pavilion in terms of the world of the Immortals and introduces the hermit who is the embodiment of an Immortal. The wayfarer is presumably Chong Ch'ol. For reasons of clarity, the translation identifies the wayfarer with the "I" narrator. In the main body of the poem, the wayfarer answers his own question by enumerating the delights of life here through the four seasons. Lines 16–25 describe the scene in spring and the busy life of the hermit. Lines 26-41 describe the scene and mood of summer, with hermit and narrator both enjoying summer delights. Lines 42-58 paint the autumn scene, with an emphasis on its idyllic nature. Lines 59–66 describe the riches of the hermit life against a winter background. The poem is rounded off with a concluding section, which features a number of themes: lines 67-74 speak of the delights of reading about the heroes of old; lines 75-84 recount the vicissitudes of the current time. The poem finishes with hermit and wayfarer sharing the wine cup and playing the *kayagum*, the Immortals' answer to the problems of the times.

The poem is conventional in that a wayfarer would hardly stay for a year and could hardly observe the four seasons simultaneously. The basic format of the poem is question and answer, but there are problems at times in identifying the speaker. Some critics bring Kim Songwon directly into the poem; they have him speak two brief sections toward the end: the passages on the delights of history and the flying Immortal. It seems best in terms of the unity of the poem, however, to take the simplest approach: to posit a single speaker, with the hermit moving in and out of the scene, an Immortal presence rather than a speaking character. This way, the contrast between the world of the Immortals and the world of the court is pointed, as is the dilemma Chong Ch'ol faces in his own life between the delights of retirement and the rewards of service. "Songsan pyolgok" is heavily Chinese and is traditionally the least highly regarded of Chong Ch'ol's *kasa*, but it has an integrated theme, which "Kwandong pyolgok" lacks.

The long *kasa*, "Kwandong pyolgok", and the series of sixteen *shijo*, "Hunmin ka", date from Chong Ch'ol's period as governor of Kangwon Province in 1580. In *Sop'o manp'il* Kim Manjung notes that "Kwandong pyolgok", "Samiin kok" and "Sokmiin kok" are all we have from antiquity of fine writing in the vernacular. "Sokmiin kok", he claims, is the finest of the three because the other two are heavily indebted to Chinese. Kim Manjung's credentials as critic supreme have never been established, yet he is the most widely quoted critical authority for Mid-Choson poetry. He is on record as saying that Hwang Chini, while an inferior poet, has her poems passed on from generation to generation because she is a woman, an opinion few contemporary scholars would accept. He gives no reasons to support his critical positions, hardly the credentials of a first-rate critic. Chong Ch'ol's *kasa* are all heavily Chinese indebted, "Sokmiin kok" admittedly less than the others, but nevertheless the Chinese influence is clear. The titles of all Chong Ch'ol's *kasa* are Chinese.

In 1555, Paek Kwanghong (1522-1556), the elder brother of the celebrated *hanshi* poet, Paek Kwanghun (1537-1592), was appointed to an official post in P'yongan Province. The appointment led to the writing of "Kwanso pyolgok" (Song of the Northwest), the first *kasa* to describe the scenery of a province. Paek's poem influenced a host of subsequent travel *kasa*, most notably Chong Ch'ol's "Kwandong pyolgok." Korean commentators traditionally place "Kwandong pyolgok" at the apex of *kasa* composition, but they have been slow to spell out the criteria that make such a high evaluation possible. The traditional high valuation of the poem, however, does much to elucidate Korean poetry attitudes both in Choson and in contemporary times. It is a testimony to the continuance of the moral stance as the heart of the Korean poetry tradition.

"Kwandong pyolgok" is a scholar-official's essay-style meditation in verse on the beauties of the Diamond Mountains and that part of the East Coast that comes under the umbrella of the

Kwandong area, in general terms from Samilp'o in North Korea to Ulchin in North Ch'ungch'ong Province. The predominant emotion is awe, an awe peppered, as one would expect from a scholar-official, with allusions to king and office, to the illustrious sages of Confucian tradition, Confucius and Mencius, to outstanding Chinese poets like Li Bai and Lim Bai, and to the great Taoist teacher Lao Zi. Although the poem does not set out to be a treatise on loyalty to the king or a primer on the qualities of a good governor, the poet, Confucian trained and surrounded by the enduring Confucian symbols of mountains and water, is constantly reminded of these considerations. The poem has some lovely descriptive passages:

1. Manp'oktong Waterfall: rainbows, dragon tails, the cacophony of the cascading waters
2. The dancing crane, vested in black and white
3. The view from Chinhyol Terrace, one mountain spur pushing north, another pushing out into the East Sea
4. The View from Kaeshim Terrace: the idea of energy and of making a hero to solve factionalism in the court
5. The Dragon Fire Pot, a particularly deep pool whose waters surge in coils to the East Sea
6. The cliff hanging in the air at Maha Gorge
7. Sunrise on Uisang Terrace at Naksan with six dragons pushing the sun up
8. The sea like a bolt of silk at Kyongp'o near Kangnung
9. The storm at sea from Manyang Terrace, seen in terms of angry whales and a silver mountain of snow and spray

These descriptive passages alone make the poem worthwhile.

The weakness of "Kwandong pyolgok" as a piece of literature is that when Chong Ch'ol has expressed his awe at natural beauty in mountain peaks and waterfalls and at man-made beauty in pagodas and terraces, he does not have much else to say. The poem lacks an integrating theme, a controlling point of view, a dramatic center of any kind. Most of all, it lacks the satirical edge and fine irony that distinguishes the best of his *shijo* poems. The poet presumably traveled with an entourage, but to all intents and purposes he is on his own, except for those brief passages when he is carried in a sedan chair. He meets no one, talks to no one, does not broaden his experience. Very often the speaker in a Ch'ong

Ch'ol *hanshi* or *shijo* is alone, but his experience is related to the experience of others and there is invariably some kind of enlargement of spirit, as for example, in the famous *shijo* about the monk crossing the bridge. There is no such enlargement in "Kwandong pyolgok". The poem remains an urbane expression of the world of a Choson dynasty bureaucrat. Kim Manjung's claim that it is one of three poems that constitute all we have from antiquity of fine writing in the vernacular will not stand up to scrutiny. Obviously Kim Manjung is not even considering *shijo*.

"Samiin kok" (Love Song) was written in 1585, the eighteenth year of the reign of Sonjo. The poet was fifty, out of office, forced home to Ch'angp'yong; his Westerner faction had been roundly defeated by the dominant Easterners. He spent his time in study, savoring the delights of retirement in nature. Despite all the protestations of harmony in nature, it was a time of intense feelings of political alienation, rejection and personal bitterness, his longest career period out of the political limelight. Kim Manjung compares "Samiin kok" and "Sokmiin kok" to the "Li sao" of Qu Yuan, a satire on the blindness of the Fair One (the king of Chu) written after the courtier, a victim of slander, was expelled from the court. Qu Yuan was a Confucian symbol of the hero, a man who championed righteousness and justice whatever the personal price. He also was a symbol of the *han* (feelings of bitterness) of the rejected courtier. Yun Sondo makes repeated references to Qu Yuan's tragic death in his celebrated *shijo* cycle *Obusashisa* (The Fisherman's Calendar). It is at the level of symbol that Qu Yuan influenced "Samiin kok" and "Sokmiin kok"; these poems do not have the shaman underpinnings that are so important to "Li sao."

The two "love" *kasa* offer problems to the interpreter. The poems are couched in words of love spoken by a woman to her beloved. These poems are allegorical, conventional. The lovers are traditionally interpreted as king and retainer, thus none of the sexual overtones associated with love poetry are permissible. And since the poet is talking about his relationship with the king, he is not at liberty to say what is really in his heart. To do so would not be very expedient politically. In such poetry one expects irony and perhaps even satire. Thus the sentiments expressed may be more complex than the traditional loyalty interpretation seems to warrant. For one thing, king and retainer were estranged, as is the couple in the poem. This inevitably breeds tension not to speak of bitterness. There were historical grounds for Chong Ch'ol to have complex feelings about his relationship with the king. His sisters married into the royal family and he himself as a boy was a regular visitor in the palace, but this did not save the family in the Ulsa purge of 1545. His father was sent into exile and his eldest brother paid the supreme price. Myongjong had been a great boyhood pal but Chong Ch'ol's relationship with Myongjong sailed in rocky seas after he refused to be lenient in the murder affair involving the king's cousin. The love *kasa* are directed to Myongjong's successor, Sonjo, who had welcomed Chong Ch'ol and other bright young men of the day into government. Ch'ong Ch'ol did well at the beginning, but factional fighting poisoned all personal relationship in government so that one wonders about the real nature of his personal feelings for the reigning monarch when the Easterners forced him home to Ch'angp'yong once again in 1585.

"Samiin kok" employs the familiar *kasa* structure of introduction, description of feelings through the seasons, and conclusion. At the beginning of the poem, the speaker – a woman - claims karma united her with her husband; she says heaven intended them to be together. Separation violates the decree of Heaven. If the metaphor applies throughout the poem, it must mean that king and retainer were also united by the decree of Heaven and that separation violates that decree. The speaker tells of her fall from grace but gives no details. The details, however, are hinted at in the companion piece "Sokmiin kok" (Love Song Continued). Her face, her actions got her in trouble, she says. Perhaps she flirted too much? What does this mean in the king-retainer relationship? It must refer to how the retainer comported himself. We know from other sources that Chong Ch'ol was often in trouble for his behavior, in particular for his involvement in factional politics and for his drinking habits. The beloved, who no longer loves the lady, has sent her away, just as the king has sent the retainer away. Her lot is sad, and time does nothing to ease her pain. Thus burdened, she recounts her sentiments of love through the four seasons. The poem runs the gamut of the rejected lover's emotions. A sense of great personal loss runs beneath the conventional expression of love and loyalty. The poem breathes an air of acceptance of a difficult fate, but one wonders how much of this is genuine. How much bitterness underlies the sentiments of love and loyalty?

In "Samiin kok" nothing is right. The speaker wakes in the spring night hoping to find her love but is disillusioned. She wonders what thoughts would fill his heart if she were to send him a plum branch. She has no reason to believe he would be anything but angry. She wonders will he accept the suit of clothes she has made for him. Presumably not. Tears fill her autumn; her winter nights are cold and miserable. The nature of the relationship precludes her from saying what is really in her heart. She does say, however, that her sickness is her beloved's fault. The poem ends with her declaration that she would be better off dead, metamorphosed into a butterfly - normally a male symbol - thus enabled to hover near her lord. The butterfly image is so common in Chinese and Korean poetry that it is close to cliché. Thus, "Samiin kok" has the weakest imaginable ending; in fact, no resolution is offered at all. On the other hand, when the king rejects the retainer, the latter is more or less helpless. The allegorical interpretation hamstrings the poet before he puts his pen to paper at all.

Contemporary critics, quoting Kim Manjung, are unanimous in their praise of "Sokmiin kok", but like their illustrious predecessor they stay clear of specifics. The poem, in fact, poses insoluble problems for the would-be interpreter or translator. There are two women speakers, referred to for convenience as A and B. The central section of the poem is at odds with any conventional sense of dialogue. It is, in fact, a lengthy monologue in which the speaker lists the trials in her quest for her beloved. In terms of dramatic unity of time and place, this section is a misfit. But then Chong Ch'ol had no knowledge of the drama. The commentators differentiate between the two speakers in character terms, finding one more concerned with herself and the other more concerned with her lord. There is general agreement that the two speakers represent facets of Chong Ch'ol himself. The sections of the poem are reasonably clear. Naming the speaker, however, of any particular section is a toss-up. Over the years the commentators have come up with every possible combination of A and B. In some scenarios, one speaker dominates; the role of the second speaker is reduced to a few lines. In other scenarios, the dialogue is shared. Whichever scenario one chooses, the underlying facts are as follows. The two speakers share one beloved. Both speakers are currently out of favor. As the poem unfolds, there is no dramatic or emotional conflict between the two speakers. In fact, they share sympathy. In the end, they find no resolution to the problem of the beloved. Thus, the drama is of a lyrical descriptive nature. The two speakers are seen as sides of one composite character, one more interested in the beloved, the other more interested in the self. Once the reader accepts that there is no conflict between the speakers, and that the speakers represent facets of one character's personality, then the allotment of lines to whichever speaker becomes secondary. At the same time, the vagueness of the allotment of roles must surely be seen as a structural weakness in the poem, unless one resorts to the traditional interpretation of the poem which sees the two women as faeries on a quest for the Fair One, to use the Li sao term. In a fairy quest construct, the two speakers can be a composite single character and the time and space problems can be easily dealt with.

The poem is ostensibly an account of two women in love with one man. However, the commentators are unanimous in declaring that there is no love interest here, no sexual context, that the poem is an allegory of the love or loyalty of a retainer for his lord. Thus the inherent dramatic content of the poem never becomes a factor, except in terms of psychological monologue, not at least until the last lines. The interpretation of the last lines suddenly becomes crucial. What is the significance of becoming a "waning" moon to shine on the beloved? Why not be a full moon? And what is the significance of becoming a nasty (*kujun*) rain as opposed to a sweet rain? It is hard to interpret a waning moon or a nasty rain as anything but negative, yet no Korean commentator makes the negative interpretation. Uniformly they posit a lady who has suffered greatly, but who is still magnanimous enough to say she will shine on her beloved in the next life and bring him increase with sweet rain. Korean poetry traditionally has interpreted its heroes and heroines in this black and white fashion. It would be so much more exciting to see Chong Ch'ol racked between feelings of love and resentment, loyalty and betrayal, to see him run the gamut of emotions in his relationship with his lord. One reading of the text sees the poem end with the docile side of Chong Ch'ol saying he will continue to serve even in the diminished role of waning moon; and the other side of his personality angrily telling the beloved to get stuffed! However, within the context of Choson society at the time, to express sentiments like these would have been the height of folly. Whither interpretation?

The commentators list five woodblock versions of *Songgang kasa*: Hwangjubon, Uisongbon, Kwanbukpon, Songjubon and Kwansabon, of which Uisongbon and Kwanbukpon have not survived.

The Hwangjubon was published in Hwangju by Yi Kyesang between 1690 and 1696. It has five *kasa*, 51 *tan'ga* (*shijo*) and an afterword by Yi Son. Because of the Yi Son afterword the text is sometimes called the Yisonbon.

The Songjubon was published in Songju in 1747 when Chong Kwana, a direct descendant of Chong Ch'ol, was magistrate of Songju. In two volumes, the first has the five *kasa* of the

Hwangjubon, and in the same order; and the second lists 79 tan'ga, with afterwords by Chong Ch'on, a great-great grandson of Chong Ch'ol, and Chong Ch'on's son Kwanha.

The Kwansobon was published in the Kwanso area in 1768 by Chong Shil, grandson of Chong Ho, who was himself the great-great grandson of Chong Ch'ol. This text lists five *kasa* and five tan'ga, with to Yi Son's afterword and a postscript by Chong Shil.

Songgang kasa: The Pine River Songs

Songgang kasa: The Pine River Songs

Untitled Shijo

> People of Kangwon Province,
> do not bring your brothers to trial.
> Servants and fields are easily acquired,
> but where
> can a brother find a brother? Don't glower
>   at each other so.

Kwanghwamun was the main gate to Kyongbok Palace, the royal palace in Seoul.

> I race through Kwanghwamun;
> I'm duty officer tonight.
> Fifth Watch: twenty-three strokes of the gong.
> Between the strokes
> remnants of the past lie like dreams.

Pongnaesan was one of the mountains where the Immortals lived. It was also the summer name for the Diamond Mountains. Here it refers to the royal palace in Seoul. Kangnam refers not to the area south of the Han River in Seoul but to Chong Ch'ol's home in Cholla Province, Ch'angp'yong.

> On Pongnaesan where my true love lives,
> the watch gong
> reverberates across the fortress, passes through the clouds, and rides the soft breeze.
> What will I do
> when I'm in Kangnam and I long to hear the sound.

> Stock from boiled bitter greens
> is tastier than meat.
> My straw hut is tiny, but it best suits my station.
> My problem
> is this longing for my love: it fills my heart with care.

Poet and scholar in the kingdom of Jin, Liu Ling was renowned for his wine drinking. Kyeham was one of Chong Ch'ol's names.

> When did Liu Ling live?
> He was a star of Chin.
> Who's this Kyeham? A lunatic from the present.
> So be it:
> What's the use in quizzing stars or lunatics?

The next two poems seem to be a pair. There are different interpretations of the text: the bran and chaff interpretation is the one given by Chong Pyong'uk in Shijo sajon. Another version interprets the phrase as meaning someone tottering from drink, meaning that if the man of the house is drunk all the time, who will you turn to for support. The first line of Listen here is not gender specific; the speaker may be addressing the man or woman of the house. The translation avoids the problem by the cryptic "Listen here" rather than something like "My good man," or "Woman of the house"

> Listen here;
> how can you live like this:
> cooking pots broken, gourds all gone?
> Need I add:
> When all you have is wheat bran and rice chaff,
> who will you turn to for support?

Poverty is not the issue here. If the speaker can be sure of love, all problems disappear. It seems best to take the speaker to be a woman. The beloved may be the king or the husband of the woman speaker. Chong Ch'ol may again be using the technique of using different characters to portray aspects of his personality and his love for the king.

> Whether I eat wheat bran or rice chaff,
> whether I have a gourd dipper or not,
> though the world falls into total disarray,
> if my lovely love
> will but love me, faith will sustain my life.

The next three poems form a group; they are a humorous dialogue with wine. The poet is the speaker in Ten years I followed you; *wine is the speaker in* If you truly hoped to achieve something, *and in* I say it once again *the poet is again the speaker. Because of vagueness in Korean with regard to pronouns, it is often difficult to decide who is speaking to whom. Other interpretations are possible.*

>Ten years I followed you
>believing I'd be an achiever.
>But you say you hate me, that I've achieved nothing.
>Perhaps
>I should write a book on temperance as a token of farewell.

>If you truly hoped to achieve something,
>would you have cultivated me from the start?
>You always seemed pleased to see me; so I followed you around.
>Now you tell me
>I'm bad: you'll have to give me up.

>I say it once again:
>I cannot live without you.
>You let me forget the bad and the bitter.
>Can I now
>discard an old friend in favor of a new love?

Human life lasts a hundred years;
of course it's a burden.
In this burdened, floating life what do you hope
  to achieve
that you tell me
you want to cut back on the cups I proffer?

Pongnaesan was a mountain in China where the Immortals dwelt; it was also the summer name for the Diamond Mountains. In poems of loyalty, however, it often refers to the royal palace in Seoul. The idea seems to be that the speaker is in the country, out of favor in the court. He longs to go back, ostensibly to see the king, but circumstances at the moment make it impossible.

If I lifted my wings
and flapped them twice or thrice,
I'd see my beloved on the highest peak of
Pongnaesan.
But what's the point
in discussing things that are impossible?

I wish to dismember my body,
to float it in the stream.
When the water reaches the shallows in the Han,
my love sickness
for my lord may find a cure.

> I'll cut out my heart
> to form a moon
> and hang brightly in a far corner of the sky.
> Then I'll go
> to my love and shine my light upon him.

Taebang Fortress is today's Namwon in North Cholla Province.

> The rise and fall of nations are myriad;
> Taebang Fortress is covered with autumn grass.
> To the herdsman's pipes I'll leave my ignorance of the past
> and I'll drink
> a cup to this great age of peace.

The speaker is again out of office, thinking back to early days in officialdom. He recalls his junior posting in the Royal Archives and remembers seeing the king. Shin Kunmang (Shin Ungshi), an official who served under Myongjong, was from Yongwol. Kunjong Gate was the south gate of Kunjong Hall.

> When Shin Kunmang was a fifth rank official
>   in the Royal Archives
> I had a sixth rank post
> with guard duties that took me outside Kunjong Gate.
> The jade face
> of my lord flickers before me.

Shady Nook Pavilion was built by Kim Songwon (1525-1597) on Mount Star. Kim Songwon is the hermit hero of Chong Ch'ol's kasa, "Songsan pyolgok."

>When the South Pole Star
>shines on Shady Nook Pavilion,
>the broad sea can repeatedly become a mulberry patch,
>but starlight
>ever renewed knows no diminishment.

The toast is offered on an occasion like a sixtieth birthday wishing the guest of honour long years. The poem has been traditionally interpreted as referring to the king. There seems to be no intrinsic evidence for this.

>That zelkova planted on the terrace,
>how long has it been growing?
>When the seedling branch is just as old,
>I'll take
>the cup and offer a toast again.

The poet longs to be restored to the bureaucracy.

>Crane, flying high
>above the clouds in the blue sky,
>do you come among us because man is so good?
>you will not fly
>away though your long feathers moult.

A Shijo Poet in the Court of King Sonjo

The komun'go is a traditional stringed instrument.

> When I strike the great string of the *komun'go*,
> My heart melts.
> Rising to the fourth string dominant I play allegro forte.
> Not a trace
> of sadness; but how can I deal with parting?

The poet longs to be restored to the bureaucracy.

> When my long feathers moult,
> I'll flap my wings again
> and soar above the cloudy blue,
> where I'll see
> a fresh, unimpeded world.

Now that I'm keeper of the state guesthouse
visitors throng this way.
Bows when they come; bows when they go; bows, bows,
    bows by the score.
One careful
look reveals it's all a dreadful bore.

Now that I'm keeper of the state guesthouse
I don my sedge cape and rain hat.
A gentle breeze angles the fine rain. I slant a fishing pole
across my shoulder,
the first of
many trips to a riverbank of red knotweed and white water
chestnut.

Pyokche was a scenic area outside Seoul.

    Now that I'm keeper of the state guesthouse
    I close the brushwood gate again.
    I throw myself among flowing waters and blue mountains;
    these I take as friends.
    Boy,
    should a caller say he's from Pyokche, tell him I'm out.

A royal tutor cried himself to death at the demise of one of the Sui kings.

> When I think of King Chang Sha's tutor
> I have to laugh.
> He took upon himself the worries of all.
> Were not sighs
> and tears enough; did he have to scream his grief as well?

> I'm aware that I'm not
> as finely featured as others.
> I've given up rouge, put aside powder.
> I have no desire
> to savour my true love's love.

A political allegory on the fate of prominent men who fall from grace.

> The tree is diseased;
> no one rests in its pavilion.
> When it stood tall and verdant, no one passed it by.
> But the leaves
> have fallen, the boughs are broken; not even birds
>   perch there now.

Yesterday I heard that Master Song
from over the hill has new wine.
I kicked the ox to its feet, threw on a saddlecloth and
 rode up here.
Boy,
is your master home? Tell him Chong Ch'ol has come.

After a ten-year interval I see again
the white jade wine cup in the Royal Academy.
The clear white sheen is as it was yesterday.
But the heart
of a man, why does it change morning and evening?

This poem deplores the confusion in the court in drafting a policy to deal with the Hideyoshi Invasion.

What happens if you pull down
beams and supports?
A host of opinions greet the leaning, skeleton house.
Carpenters
with rulers and ink keep milling around.

Holding back a horse laugh
brings a tickle to my nose.
Forced coquetry, I fear, destroys the fullness of love.
Until the sweet wine
matures, better not flirt with affection.

No moaning, please,
about who's staying and who's going.
No horse laughs, please, about who's drunk and who's sober.
Is it so terrible
to throw off your cape on a rainy day?

We'll strain sour wine and drink
until we can't abide the taste.
We'll boil bitter greens and chew until they become sweet.
We'll stay
on the road until the nails that hold the heels to our clogs
        are worn away.

A tall Shilla pagoda,
eight hundred years old,
resonates to the successive strokes of the great metal bell,
highlighting
the twilight view across the field of a solitary mountain pavilion.

A sudden shower
splatters the lotus leaf,
but I cannot find the track of water.
I wish my heart
were like that leaf, that nothing ever stained it.

Where has the crane gone;
the pavilion is empty.
Were I to disappear so, when would I return?
Come or go,
I'll drink a cup of wine.

I'll wash and rewash
my lowly raw silk jacket,
dry it in sunlight, iron it again and again,
then drape it
over the buoyant shoulders of my love.

Somewhere on Namsan Mountain
Scrivener Ko has built his straw hut.
He has given it flowers and a moon, rocks and water.
Even wine
he has provided, and he's asked me to visit.

My old loves are still my loves,
yesterday's amours are today's.
When I think of it, it's all a dream; old traces are all that remain.
When old affections
are unchanged, there's no reason to turn away.

I'm fifty now, no longer young:
yet wherever I go, at the mere sight of wine,
I break into a broad toothy grin. Why, why?
Wine is an old,
old acquaintance; I can never forget him.

My carelessness
has been there from the start.
Things left thoughtlessly to chance can prove serious.
I wake
and turn away; there's real cause for alarm.

Shall I put my worries aside
and sigh after another's smiles?
Shall I put my cup aside and join another club?
What can change
the pristine jade-like quality of my heart?

Don't waken babies from sweet sleep;
infants invariably cry.
Babies fight for the breast; don't fuss about it, with a
"Who's this child,
or who's that? It's unbecoming on an adult's lips.

Forty thousand boxes of bright jewels
caught in the lotus leaves.
Gathered, measured, where shall I send them?
Pattering drops,
they are so vibrantly gay!

Somehow or other
my time has almost gone.
Bustling, shoving; what have I achieved?
So be it:
people keep saying, "Enough, enough!" What can I do
       but enjoy myself?

As I move the goosefoot forward
the great string of the *komun'go* resounds,
like water once ice-bound bursting now from its stream.
Somewhere
rain falls on lotus leaves; is it trying to match the sound?

The falling paulownia leaves
tell me it's autumn
A fine rain falls in the clear river; the night air has an edge.
I parted from
my love 1,000 *li* away: I fear I'll get no sleep tonight.

I've been gone such a very long time;
leaves fly in the autumn wind.
Ice and snow melt; it's time for spring flowers to bloom.
I have no news
of my love: this makes me sad.

The peach paradise is the royal court and the clouds are the evil officials that brought about the poet's banishment.

>Clouds shrouded
>the peach paradise last night.
>A brace of lovely phoenix vied in dalliance.
>Why search
>for feathers that fell among men?

>When our droopy-eared horse
>goes for a load of salt,
>anyone can tell he's good for a thousand <u>li</u>.
>Why is it
>the men of today think of him only as fat?

This song is directed to a paper kite. The ascription is doubtful. Kwon P'il's Sokchu chip records a Chinese version.

>Take all the misfortunes
>of our household,
>drop them not on men; hang them on a tree.
>In wind and wet
>they'll fade naturally away.

Songgang kasa: The Pine River Songs

Poems proclaiming loyalty to the king were often couched in the language of a lover to his beloved.

> Snow falling in the pine forest,
> every branch a flower.
> I'll cut a branch and send it to my love.
> If my love
> but see it first, what matter though it melt?

> A shadow is reflected in the water:
> a monk is crossing the bridge.
> Monk, stay a moment; let me ask you where you're going?
> Stick pointed
> at white clouds, he passes without a backward glance.

Paduk *(Go) is a very popular board game.*

> The lad has gone to dig fernbrake;
> the bamboo grove is empty.
> Who will pick up the pieces scattered across the *paduk* board?
> Reclined
> against a pine tree root, inebriate, I do not feel the approach of day.

There are different interpretations of the Chinese term, which is pronounced soksa in Korean. Chong Pyong'uk says it means ordinary; other commentators say it means a worldling. The worldling interpretation seems at odds with the speaker's heart.

>Were I brilliant,
>my love would not forsake me.
>Better be ordinary, for then I could stroll with my love.
>Not even
>being ordinary, I fear I'll never see my love.

This poem, sometimes attributed to Yu Huiryong (1480-?), is structurally unusual: the first part of the final chang (line 4) has only two syllables.

>Butterflies hover in pairs where flowers blossom thick;
>orioles perch in pairs on the branches of green willows.
>Flying creatures, crawling creatures, all are in pairs.
>Tell me,
>why am I alone without a mate?

>Pearly raindrops on green hills,
>how can you deceive me?
>Sedge rain cape and horsehair hat, how can you deceive me?
>Two days ago
>I took off my silk robes; now nothing soilable remains.

Sleep bound birds fly home;
the new moon rises.
"Monk," I cry, to the lone figure crossing
   the single-log bridge:
"How far to
your temple? I can hear the beating of the drum."

The evening sun slants low;
river and sky are a single hue.
Wildgoose, crying for autumn leaves and reed flowers,
the season's
done and still I have no news of my love!

Two stone Buddhas, naked and fasting,
face each other on the road.
Exposed to wind, rain, snow, and frost they may be,
but of human
parting they know nothing! For this I envy them.

Husband dead;
tears flow down my breasts.
Milk salted; the infant frets.
What sort of man
would ask me to be his?

Where is that boat going,
buffeted by stormy seas?
Black clouds are bundled in the sky; why did it sail?
Be careful,
sailors of fragile craft!

Why does that pine tree stand
so near the road?
I wish it stood a little back, perhaps in the hollow behind.
Everyone
geared with rope and axe will want to cut it down.

Kangho, translated here simply as water, is a reference to a district in China with three rivers and five lakes mentioned in a poem by Du Fu (712-70). It describes the world of a hermit.

> White gull,
> floating on the water,
> it was an accident my spit hit you on the back.
> White gull,
> don't be angry: I spat because the world is a dirty place.

> When did the leaves come out,
> already they're falling in the autumn breeze.
> The ice and snow have melted, spurring spring flowers into bloom.
> No news yet
> from my love. I am greatly saddened.

The poem is built around a pun on Chin'ok (genuine jade), the name of a kisaeng who had an intimate relation with Chong Ch'ol.

> Genuine jade, they said;
> I thought it mere imitation.
> Now that I see it, I must admit, it is indeed pure jade.
> I have
> a fleshly awl and with it I will drill.

Qu Yuan was banished as a result of palace intrigue in old China. He died by drowning. The reference here is to his loyal heart.

>Fishermen of the Chu River,
>do not fish these waters.
>Qu Yuan's bitterness is in the bellies of the fish.
>You can boil
the fish, but you can't boil out the loyalty of Qu Yuan's heart.

>I promised to return to rivers and lakes,
>but I've had ten busy years.
The white gulls, unaware of the facts, chide me for being late,
>but the king's
>favor is so precious, I must repay it before I go back.

>When the paulownia leaves fell
>I knew it was autumn.
>A fine drizzle falls on the blue river: the night air is chilly.
>I left my love
>a thousand *li* away; I cannot sleep tonight.

Songgang kasa: The Pine River Songs

Hunmin ka (Instructing the People)

Hunmin ka is a series of sixteen didactic shijo *written by Chong Ch'ol when he was governor of Kangwon Province.*

Father's Honour; Mother's Affection

> My father gave me birth,
> my mother sustenance.
> Without father and mother, would I have life?
> How can I
> repay a favor that is boundless as Heaven?

King and Subject

> The relationship between king and people
> is the same as that between heaven and earth.
> Since the king would feign know our plight,
> how can we,
> the people, eat the succulent parsley by ourselves.

Respect between Brothers

> Big brother, little brother,
> touch each other's flesh.
> Who gave you birth? You are so alike.
> Suckled at
> the same breast, don't harbour divided hearts.

Filial Piety

>While your parents are alive,
>do all that filial piety requires.
>It's too late for regret when they go.
>Filial piety
>is one service you can't then provide, though you try
>for the rest of your life.

Grace between Spouses

>Husband and wife
>are one body in two,
>meant to grow old together, to go in death together.
>Why, then,
>does that doting old fool glare at me so?

Distinction between the Sexes

>A man turns aside from the road
>a woman walks;
>and a woman turns aside from the road a man walks.
>So ask not
>the name of one who is neither husband nor wife.

Songgang kasa: The Pine River Songs

Educating Children

>Your son is reading the Book of Filial Piety;
>how much has he learned?
>In a few days my son will finish the Book of Rites.
>When our children
>complete these books, will they attain wisdom?

Etiquette among Villagers

The kat *is the traditional Korean horsehair hat; the cowl is the monk's cowl.*

>Village people,
>let's do what is right.
>A man born into this world who doesn't do what is right
>   is like
>   a horse or a cow being fed with a *kat* and cowl
>   on its head?

Order between Old and Young

>If an elder takes you by the wrist,
>offer both hands to help him to his feet.
>If he has to go out, follow him with a walking stick.
>After the village festival
>make sure he gets safely home.

Trust between Friends

>In the world of men is there anything
>more trustworthy than a friend?
>A friend points out all my faults.
>Without such friends,
>would I be a complete man?

Family Support in Poverty and Calamity

>Ah, nephew! Nothing to eat;
>what will you do?
>Ah, poor man! Nothing to wear; what will you do?
>Speak up about
>things that are amiss! I want to take care of you.

Mutual Help in Marriage and Death

>How are you managing
>the bereavements in your house?
>When will you get your daughter a husband?
>I don't have
>much myself, but I'd like to help.

Songgang kasa: The Pine River Songs

Farm the Land and Cultivate Silkworms Assiduously

      It's full daylight now;
      let's take our hoes and go.
      When I finish my fields, I'll help you weed yours.
      On the way back
      we'll pick mulberry leaves and feed the silkworms.

Do Not Steal

      Though you go without clothes yourself,
      don't filch the clothes of another.
Though you go without food yourself, don't beg the food of
      another.
      Stained once
      it's hard to get washed clean again.

No Gambling: No Litigation

      Don't play dice or chess;
      don't write litigation writs.
If your family is ruined, what will you do? You could become
      someone's enemy?
      Don't you know
it's the nation makes the laws and decides what's right and wrong.

Don't Let an Old-timer Carry a Burden on the Road

>Old-timer, burdened head and back,
>give me your load.
>I'm young; not even stones are heavy.
>It's bad enough
>to be old without bearing extra baggage.

Songgang kasa: The Pine River Songs

Sasol shijo *or* kasa

Changjinju sa (An Inducement to Imbibe)

Commentators debate whether this is a sasol *(extended)* shijo *or a* kasa. *The* jiggy *is an A-frame, a wooden carrying frame strapped to the bearer's back.*

Let's drink a cup of wine; let's drink another!
With petals from flowers we've cut, let's mark our cups; let's drink and drink, let's drink forever!
For when at last this body dies, it will be wrapped in a straw mat and strapped to a *jiggy*, or, perhaps, it will be borne on an elegantly decked bier, ten thousand standard bearers shedding tears. Either way, once among the reeds and rushes, the oaks and willows, when the sun is yellow and the moon is white, when fine rain falls or thick snowflakes flurry, when whirlwinds blow a mournful dirge, who will offer me a cup?
Need I add:
when monkeys whistle on my grave, won't it be too late for regrets?

Kasa

Samiin kok (Love Song)

I followed you
    into this world.
Karma bound us for a lifetime;
    Heaven had to know.
My youth for you; your love for me;
    heart and love without peer.
All we wished
    was a lifetime together;
now old age finds us
    apart and full of longing.
It seems like only yesterday I served you;
    I lived in the Moon Palace.[5]
Subsequently,
    I fell in the world.
My hair, once well combed,
    is three years in tangles.
Powder and rouge I have, but for whom
    do I make myself beautiful?
My tribulations
    are bundled high like mountain folds.
I sigh,
    I cry.
Life has limits;
    tribulations are limitless.
Time, insensible as always,
    flows by like water.
Hot, cold; the seasons come and go;
    they know their term;
I listen, I look;
    there is so much to feel.

---

[5] Kwanghan chon is the palace on the moon; here the reference is to the royal palace in Seoul.

Suddenly spring breezes blow;
    they melt the piled snow.
Outside the window, two, three branches
    of the plum burst into flower.
Essence of coolness; how can I describe
    the subtle fragrance?
The dawn moon
    shines on my pillow.
I am filled with joy.
    Is it my love, is it not?
Oh to cut that plum branch
    and send it to my love!
What thoughts would fill his heart
    at sight of you?

Petals fall, new leaves sprout:
    there's a carpet of green.
Screens are desolate,
    embroidered hangings mask emptiness.
I roll up the lotus curtain,
    set out the peacock screen.[6]
I am filled with tribulation;
    the day is interminable.
I cut a bolt of mandarin duck silk,
    unravel the five-colored thread,
measure the cloth with a golden rule.
    A suit for my love!
My seamstress skills are unparalleled;
    the suit is elegance itself.
I put it in a white jade box upon a jiggy [7]
    done in mother-of-pearl.

---

[6] The peacock screen in Shu China had the power to bewitch a man into marriage.
[7] An A-frame carrier.

I must send this suit to my love.
　　I look to where he lives.
Mountains, clouds –
　　the road is rough beyond words.
A thousand, ten thousand *li*!
　　Who would travel such a path?
Were someone to go, would my love open the box
　　and greet the suit as he greets me?

In the space of a night, there's frost in the air;
　　honking geese are on the wing.
I climb alone to the high pavilion
　　and roll up the bead curtain.
The moon rises on East Mountain;
　　I see the Pole Star.
Is it my love? Tears of joy spurt
　　involuntarily from my eyes.
Oh to grab the bright moonbeams,
　　to send them to the Phoenix Pavilion![8]
My love could hang them on the pavilion,
　　light up the eight corners of the world,
make bright as day every remote village,
　　every rugged mountain valley.

Heaven and earth are without pulse;
　　white snow lies everywhere.
Men can't move;
　　birds can't fly.
When it's as cold as this
　　south of the Xiao and the Xiang,[9]
no need to speak of the Jade Pavilion[10]
　　in the high places of the north!

---

[8] The royal palace.
[9] Two rivers in China.
[10] The royal palace.

Oh to raise the warm breath of spring,
    to warm my love where he lives;
to send the bright sunlight from the eaves
    of my thatched house to the Jade Pavilion.
Dressed in scarlet skirt,
    blue sleeves rolled half way up,
I lean on my bamboo stick
    in the setting sun:
I have much to think about.
    The short sun soon goes down;
I sit stiffly
    through the long night.
I put out the lamp, put down
    the inlaid harp, recline.
Chin cupped in my hands, I wonder
    will I see my love in dreams.
The duck embroidered quilt is cold;
    when will this interminable night end?

Through the twelve divisions of the day,
    through the thirty days of the month.
I think, I think, I think;
    I try to forget my tribulations,

but sorrow is so embedded
    it pierces to the bone;
ten physicians renowned as Bianque [11]
    could not cure my sickness.
Ah, this sickness
    is my love's doing.
Better die,
    become a tiger butterfly;

---

[11] A famous physician from the Warring Dynasties in China.

A Shijo Poet in the Court of King Sonjo

perch on flower branch
   after flower branch,
fly with scented wings
   to my love's coat.
My love may not know me,
   but I can follow him around.

Sokmiin kok (Love Song Continued)

  Lady hasting on your way,
   I know your face.
  How come you've left
   the palace of the Lord of Heaven?
  The sun is almost down:
   whom are you rushing to meet?
  Ah, good friend, it's you;
   listen to my story.
  My face, my actions
   caused me to lose the king's favor.
  Once he greeted me
   with warmth.
  I trusted him;
   I had no other thought.
  Perhaps my flirting
   got on his nerves;
  the light of his countenance
   in greeting darkened.
  In bed the problem filled my mind;
   sitting up I sought answers.
  My sins were piled
   high as mountains.
  Why resent Heaven;
   why blame men?
  Bleakly I tried to unravel the conundrum:
   it was the Creator's fault!

Don't think such thoughts, good friend.
    I'm eaten up myself inside.
When I served My Lord,
    I knew his affairs.
He's delicate as water,
    how long can he prevail?
How will he fare in the cold of spring,
    in the heat of summer?
Who will care for him
    in autumn and winter?
Does he enjoy his morning porridge,
    his breakfast and dinner as of yore?
Does he sleep through
    the interminable winter night?
I long for news
    of my Lord's household.
The sun has gone today.
    Will someone have news tomorrow?
I have nowhere to trust my heart.
    Where can I go?
I push my way
    up a steep hill,
grabbing trees and rocks
    as I go.
It's a world
    of cloud and mist.
Hills and streams are dark;
    I cannot see sun or moon.

Songgang kasa: The Pine River Songs

When I cannot see
   in front of my nose,
how can I hope to see
   a thousand *li*?
Better go to the waterside
   and check the boats.
Wind and waves
   dizzy the river.
The boatmen are gone;
   empty boats are tied to the shore.
I stand alone on the bank
   and watch the setting sun;
news of My Lord's house
   seems even more remote.

Returning in the night
   to the cold bedding of my thatched hut,
I wonder for whom
   the lamp on the wall brightens.
Up, down,
   my heart is in constant crisis;
Strength fails,
   suddenly I fall into a light sleep.
Devotion stirs profoundly;
   I see my lord in dream.
Already his jade fair face
   is middle-aged.
I try to uncover
   the thought hidden in his heart.
Tears pour out;
   it is impossible to speak.

A catch in the throat
   stops all baring of the heart.
The cry of the unruly cock
   awakens me from sleep.
Ah, all is futile!
   Where is my lord?
Suddenly I get to my feet,
   sit back again,
open the window,
   look outside;
a sad shadow
   is all that follows me around.
Better to be a waning moon
   and shine inside his window.

Lady, forget about the moon:
   be a nasty rain instead.

Kwandong pyolgok (Song of the East Coast)

> Reclined in the bamboo grove,
> > victim of my love for rivers and streams. [12]
> Big news! I am to be Governor of Kwandong, [13]
> > all eight hundred *li*.
> The king's favor
> > knows no limits!

> I race on horseback
> > through Long Autumn Gate, [14]
> take my leave of the king
> > and set out on my way,
> eyes trained on
> > the Gate of Feasts, [15]
> the king's jade tally [16]
> > my standard.

> Change horses at P'yonggu Posthouse, [17]
> > follow the Black River. [18]
> Where is Toad River? [19]
> > That's Pheasant Ridge. [20]
> Where do the slow-flowing waters
> > of the Soyang River drain?
> An aging retainer leaving the capital
> > faces the prospect of white hair.

---

[12] The term used here '*kangho*' refers to a district in China with three rivers and five lakes found in a poem by Tu Fu; it describes the secluded world of someone who has retired from public life.

[13] Kwandong is the ancient eastern province, stretching from Yoju to the East Coast. From Seoul to P'yonghae at the far end of Kangwon Province was 800 *li*.

[14] Yonch'u mun, west gate, Kyongbok Palace.

[15] Kyonghoe mun, the gate south of Kyonghoe Pavilion in Kyongbok Palace.

[16] Symbol of office given by the king to the new appointee.

[17] Literally flat-hill posthouse, some 20 miles east of Yangju. The road forked here, one road going to Ch'unch'on, the other going to Wonju.

[18] Som kang, a river in Yoju.

[19] A tributary of the Han river southwest of Wonju.

[20] Ch'iak san near Wonju.

After a night in Ch'orwon,
    I climb at first light to Pukkwan Pagoda.
Thought I might see
    the highest peak of Capital Mountain. [21]
Magpies scrawk
    on the site of Kungye's palace:
in knowledge or ignorance, I wonder,
    of the waxing and waning of old time?
Hoeyang shares its name
    with a village in the ancient kingdom of Han.
Will I see again the noble mien
    of Prefect Ji Zhangru? [22]
All's well in the official residence.
    It's the third month.
Hwach'on Stream stretches
    to the Diamond Mountains.
I cast off all accoutrements;
    lighten my load.
Stick in hand I set out
    along the narrow stony track.
Hundred Stream Canyon [23] is on one side
    as I approach Ten Thousand Falls. [24]
I see a silver-white rainbow
    and a jade-tailed dragon.
Coils, swirls,
    the spew explodes for miles around;
thunder in the ear,
    snow in the eye.

---

[21] Samgak san, literally triangle or three horn mountain; here it refers to Kun'gye's capital. Kun'gye set up the short-lived kingdom of Later Koguryo.

[22] Famed governor of Hoeyang in Han China. Hoeyang was also an old name for Ch'orwon.

[23] Paekch'ondong, north-east of Changan-sa Temple, where Ma Ui, the last prince of Shilla, was said to have retired.

[24] Manp'oktong, the valley stretching below P'yohun-sa Temple.

On the top story of Diamond Terrace, [25]
    the immortal crane has strung a rope,
awakened perhaps from first sleep
    by the jade flute tones of the spring breeze.
White blouse, black skirt,
    the crane soars into the sky
in a revel of joy
    with the master of West Lake. [26]

I look down at twin peaks:
    Great Incense Burner and Small Incense Burner; [27]
climb again to Real Rest Terrace [28]
    behind True Sun Temple.
I sit and rest.
    I can see the true face of Lu Shan. [29]
The Creator has made
    a great confusion.
What flies should not run;
    what stands should not soar;
studded with lotus, tied with jade;
    spur to the East Sea, pillar to the north sky.
High View Terrace [30] and solitary Hyolmang Peak [31]
    rise high as if to ask a question of the sky,
staunch through all the kalpas.
    Ah where is there your like?
Back up on Open the Heart Terrace, [32]
    I look out at Many Fragrance Fortress. [33]
I try to count the 12,000 peaks,
    every peak, every rock edge draped in primeval energy.

---

[25] Kumgang tae, a high terrace north of P'yohun-sa Temple.
[26] West Lake was a famed beauty spot in China. Lin Bu of Song lived there; he loved the crane as a son and the plum as a wife.
[27] So hyangno and Tae hyangno, two peaks at the entrance to Manp'oktong.
[28] Chinhol Terrace is a high terrace at the back of Chongyang-sa Temple.
[29] Mountain in China famous for its beauty. The quotation is from Su Dongpo.
[30] Mango tae, a high cliff.
[31] Hyolmang pong, literally hole-view-peak, has an aperture half way up.
[32] Kaeshim Terrace, above Chongyang-sa Temple.
[33] Chunghyang Fortress, a white cliff face, looks like a folding screen.

The clear vitality is what surprises.
 I wish I could contrive a hero from this
 energy.
In terms of form the possibilities are myriad;
 each peak is different.
These peaks are unchanged
 since the world came into being.
Seeing them now for the first time,
 my heart fills with a multitude of feelings.

Who climbed
 the pinnacle of Piro Peak? [34]
Was East Mountain higher,
 was Grand Mountain higher? [35]
How could I know
 that the kingdom of Lu was small,
that the world under the broad expanse
 of heaven was tiny.
How could I plumb
 the mystery of what I saw?
I couldn't get to the top;
 would going back down be a problem?

I approach Lion Peak [36]
 by way of Wont'ong valley.[37]
A broad cliff
 is the site of the Dragon's Firepot.
The old dragon of a thousand years
 lies in coils within.
Day and night the coils unwind
 taking him to the broad sea.
When will he gather wind and cloud
 for a three-day rain? [38]

---

[34] Piro pong is the highest peak in the Diamond Mountains.

[35] Two mountains in China. Mencius writes that when Confucius climbed East Mountain he thought the Kingdom of Lu was small; and when he climbed Grand Mountain, he thought the whole world was small.

[36] Saja Peak takes its name from a rock on the cliff face shaped like a lion. It lies north of the Dragon's Firepot.

[37] Not the Wont'ong outside Injae. This Wont'ong Valley is in North Korea.

Please save the grasses
   that have withered in the shade.
After Maha Gorge [39] and the exquisite rock carving,[40]
   I cross Goose Gate Hill, [41]
climb up to Buddha's Terrace [42]
   by the rotten single log bridge.
A thousand feet of sheer cliff
   stand in the air.
Slowly I count
   the strands of the Milky Way;
warp and woof,
   it hangs there on the loom.
Twelve strands the book says.[43]
   To me, there are more.
Had Li Bai
   the chance to talk it out,
he'd never have claimed
   Lushan was lovelier than here.
So much for mountain country;
   it is time to head for the East Sea .
I get on a small sedan chair
     and begin the slow ascent to Mountain Glow Pagoda. [44]
The imposing green valley
   and the birds chirping in various voices
seem to resent
   farewell.
I unfold the banner
   in a flutter of five colors;
Flute and drum mingle in performance;
   the clouds seem to lift from the sea.

---

[38] The reference is to a sweet rain, a metaphor for good government, in a poem by the Chinese poet Su Shi.
[39] Maha yon, the deepest gorge in Manp'okdong, site of a temple built by the great Shilla monk, Uisang.
[40] A beautiful rock carving of Maitreya close to Maha Gorge.
[41] Anmun jae (Goose Gate Hill), between Maha Gorge and Yujom-sa Temple.
[42] Pulchong Terrace.
[43] Sansudo kyong, a book on natural features of the landscape.
[44] Sanyong nu (Mountain Glow Pagoda), the gate pavilion to Yujom-sa Temple.

My horse, sure-footed on the shining sands,
    an inebriate immortal slumped in the saddle,
passes among the flowering sea-roses
    that border the boundless sea,
White gull, fly not away.
    Don't you know I'm a friend?

I examine Golden Orchid Cave, [45]
    continue up to Stone Pillar Pavilion. [46]
Four columns stand,
    all that remains of White Jade Pavilion. [47]
Was it built by a master craftsman,
    or by the hammer of a god?
What in fact
    do the six faces signify?

I forgo Kosong
    and move on to Samilp'o. [48]
The red letters are clearly etched;
    where are the four Immortals? [49]
After their four-day sojourn,
    where did they go?
Are they at Immortals at Play Pool, [50]
    at Bright Prince Lake? [51]
Where did they sit?
    Clear Torrent Pavilion,[52] Multi-vista Terrace? [53]

---

[45] Kumnan kul, a cave in a high cliff by the sea.

[46] Ch'ongsok Pagoda, one of the eight sights of Kwandong, a series of columns rising from the sea, four of which supported the pagoda.

[47] Paegok Pavilion, where the jade emperor lived. The reference is to a Li Bai poem.

[48] On the hill north of Samilp'o, six Chinese characters are carved into the rock: "The men of Yongnang are going south."

[49] The four Immortals are four Shilla *hwarang* who reputedly took a pleasure trip to Samilp'o.

[50] Sonyu Pool, south of Kansong.

[51] Yongnang Lake, south of Kansong.

[52] Ch'onggan Pavilion, south of Kansong.

[53] Man'gyong Terrace, east of Chonggang Pavilion.

Pear blossoms fall;
  the sad song of the scops-owl fills the air.
I sit on Uisang Terrace, [54]
  on the hill east of Naksan;
I rise in the night
  to see the sunrise.
Propitious clouds blossom,
  six dragons take the strain;
the sun rises from the sea;
  the heavens tremble.
The sun climbs into the sky;
  bright enough to count its golden locks.
Will passing clouds
  screen the light?
Where is the Immortal poet? [55]
  Does only the poem remain?
Between heaven and earth
  news of a great poet lives on.

Over the azaleas
  of High Ridge Mountain, [56]
the feather-top carriage
  rolls down to Kyongp'o as the sun declines.
Ten *li* of sheer-ice silk,
  ironed and ironed again,
stretched among
  the great spreading pines,
water so calm
  I can count the grains of sand.
A lone boat sails past;
  I go up to the pagoda.

---

[54] Terrace overlooking the sea at Naksan-sa Temple.
[55] The reference is to Li Bai.
[56] Hyonsan, in the north of Yangyang County.

The great sea stretches out
 from River Gate Bridge. [57]
So peaceful! Such atmosphere!
 An unbounded world!
Where
 is there richer store!
I could recount
 the tale of Hongjang. [58]
Kangnung famed for virtue
 and cultural accomplishment.
Gates commemorating fidelity and filial deeds
 dot the valleys.
Lines of houses,
 each rating a ranking post.

West Bamboo Pavilion, [59]Pearl Posthouse: [60]
 underneath, the waters of fifty streams
carry the shadow of the Taebaek Mountains
 to the East Sea. [61]
Would that they flowed by the Han River
 to the slopes of Namsan in Seoul.
But this is an official trip, circumscribed.
 And I can't say I dislike the scene.
Pleasant thoughts fill the heart;
 no room for the traveller's sadness.
Should I float off on the raft of the Immortals,
 head for the Great Dipper and the Herdboy?
Should I seek the Immortals
 in Cinnabar Cave? [62]
I have not seen to the root of the sky;
 Regretfully, I climb to Mangyang Pavilion.[63]

---

[57] Kangmun kyo, a wooden bridge at the eastern entrance to Kyongp'o, the beach near Kangnung.
[58] The reference is to the love affair between Pak Shin, a royal inspector, and Hongjang a well-known Kangnung *kisaeng*.
[59] Chukso Pavilion, situated on a cliff south of Chinju (Pearl) Posthouse. One of the eight sights of Kwandong.
[60] Chinju Posthouse, in Samch'ok. Chinju was an old name for Samch'ok.
[61] The T'aebaek mountains are the backbone of Korea.
[62] Tanhyol, a cave in Kosong County visited by the four *hwarang* Immortals.
[63] Mangyang Pavilion in P'yonghae County is one of the eights sights of

The sky lies beyond the sea;
    what stretches beyond the sky?
The whales are angry enough;
    who frightened them to blow and spume in tumult?
It's as if a silver mountain were levelled
    and the Immortals were sporting at play.
How else explain the white snow
    that fills the width of the fifth month sky?

Night falls before I know it;
    wind and waves quiet down.
At a spot near where the sun rises,
    I await the rising of the moon.
A long length of propitious light appears,[64]
    then hides in the clouds.
I raise the bead curtain again,
    sweep the jade steps again;
Straight-backed I watch
    until the Morning Star rises.
Someone has sent
    a single spray of white lotus.
Would that I could show
    this wonder world to all men.
I pour a glass of divine nectar,
    offer it to the moon and ask:
Where have all the heroes gone?
    Who were the four Immortals?
I would have news of the old world
    from anyone who comes.
The road stretches from Immortals Mountain
    along the East Sea.

Kwandong.
[64] Reference to a poem by Su Dongpo (1037-1101)

I pillow on a pine root,
    fall into a light sleep.
A man appears to me in my dreams.
    He says:
I know you;
    you are a ranking Immortal in heaven.
You misread a character
    in the Book of the Yellow Court [65]
and came down
    into the world of men.
Stay a moment;
    drink this cup of wine.
He dips with the Great Dipper,
    fills the cup with water from the sea,
drinks himself and gives me to drink,
    four cups in all.
A flower breeze gently blows,
    lifting my by the armpits.
A little more and I would float
    into the broad expanse of heaven.
"Take this wine,
    divide it among the four seas;
and when you have rendered
    the numberless millions inebriate,
we'll meet again
    and have another cup."
When he finishes speaking,
    he mounts a crane and rides into the broad sky.

The jade flute screels in the sky;
    is it yesterday or the day before?

---

[65] A Taoist scripture composed by Lao Zi. An Immortal is said to have misread a character in the Book of the Yellow Court in the presence of the Jade Emperor and to have been banished to earth as a result.

I wake from sleep
  and look down at the sea.
I do not know the depth of the sea,
  how could I know its width?
(Dip, dip it all,
  pour, pour it all.
Boy, rinse the cup;
  bring a drink
to all who dwell in the Nine Heavens;
  make everyone merry.) [66]
There is no mountain in the world
  where the moon does not shine.

---

[66] The section in brackets is found only in the *Hyopryul taesong* text; it is not in the *Songjubon* or the *Isonbon*.

Songsan pyolgok (Song of Mount Star)

    A wayfarer,
        lodged on Mount Star: I said:
    Master of Soha Hall's Shady Nook Pavilion,[67]
        listen to me.
    With so many fine things
        in the world of men,
    why does age tie you
        to one river, one mountain;
    you come into this mountain retreat,
        you don't leave?

    I swept the pine root again,
        put a cushion on the bamboo settle,
    Popped up, sat down,
        tried it out for comfort.
    The clouds in the sky
        were wonder stones[68] of the house;
    the master
        flitted in and out.
    The blue stream, flecked with white,
        swept around the pavilion,
    as if someone had stolen
        Chiknyo's [69] weave
    and unrolled the silk
        in a flowing riot of pattern.
    There's no calendar in the hills,
        no way to tell the passage of time.
    The scene before me
        has a face for every season.

---

[67] Soha tang and Shig'yong chong, a house and pavilion on Mount Star built by Kim Songwon. He presented the pavilion to his father-in-law Im Okryong.

[68] A reference perhaps to Sosok (Auspicious Stone) Terrace on Mudung Mountain, near Kwangju.

[69] Chiknyo and Kyonu, the legendary ill-starred lovers (Altair and Vega) who got together once a year. Chiknyo's weave is the Milky Way.

What I see, what I hear
   is the Immortals' world.
Morning sunlight shines on my plum window;
   I waken to the fragrance.
An old mountain man
   has no shortage of things to do.
In a sunny spot under the hedge
   he plants his cucumber;
he weeds, he scuffles,
   he tends them in the rain.
The old story of Blue Gate [70]
   is re-enacted.
I tie my straw sandals,
   set out with bamboo staff.
Peach blossoms line the path by the stream
   right down to the fragrant grasses by the water.
The shadow of the stonewall screen[71],
   reflected like a painting in a brightly polished mirror,
I take as a friend
   as we go down together to West Stream.
This is paradise,
   the Peach Blossom Paradise.

The South Wind springs up,
   scattering the green shade.
The oriole knows the season;
   where did it come from?
I nod off on Emperor Xi's [72] pillow,
   waken a moment later.

---

[70] The Blue Gate was the south-east gate of Zhangan. The story is told that after the fall of Qin, Shao Ping put on hemp and lived in poverty raising cucumbers on the east side of Zhangan. The cucumbers were arrayed in five colors, very beautiful to see. The people called them the Blue Gate fruit.

[71] The screen is a cliff.

[72] A legendary Chinese king, Fu Xi (Pokhui in Korean). The pillow is a symbol of peaceful times.

The balustrade, wet from the air,
   floats in the water.
I don my hemp coat,
   slant my kudzu hat,
contort my back
   to get a look at the fish.
The night's rain has prompted
   the red and white lotus to a fused blooming.
The whole mountain
   is fragrant in the still air.
It's as if I were face to face with Zhou Tunyi, [73]
   asking him about the ultimate principle,
as if the Immortals in Heaven
   had unfolded the jade character before my eyes.
I'm looking across at Noja Rock,
   Small Purple Rapids are to one side.
The spreading pine is my sunshade;
   I sit down on the stony road.
In the world of men it's summer;
   here it's autumn.
Ducks that floated on blue river water
   have flown over to sit on white sands.
Friends with the white gulls,
   they sleep as if time were an irrelevance,
so unwittingly at leisure
   they remind me of the master here.
In the Fourth Watch, the moon rises
   between the leaves of the paulownia;
a thousand cliffs, ten thousand gorges
   are clear as day.
Who moved the Crystal Palace
   from lakeside?

---

[73] Famous Song dynasty Neo-Confucian philosopher.

It's as if I had jumped across the Milky Way
    and landed in the Moon Palace.
I push off from the fishing hole
    at Twin Old Pines,
let the boat drift at will
    in the current.
Red knotweed and white pondweed
    line the river bank as I pass.
Blue Ring Hall[74] and the Dragon's Pool check
    are right in front of the boat.
Boys feeding cattle
    in the green of the river bank,
intoxicated by the mood,
    play the short flute.
The dragon in the riverbed
    may waken and surface at any moment;
herons, prodded by the mist,
    may abandon their nests and take to the air.
Su Dongpo's Red Cliff
    praises the seventh month;
everyone agrees on the glory
    of the fifteenth day of the eighth month.[75]
Feather clouds are everywhere;
    the water completely calm;
The moon in the sky
    sits on top of the pine.
Remember Li Bai who drowned
    trying to grab that moon.

---

[74] Hwanbyok tang (Blue Ring Hall) was built by Kim Yunche on a hill overlooking Ch'anggye Stream opposite Mount Star. Kim Yunche was Chong Ch'ol's wife's maternal grandfather. He dreamed a dragon dream, met the youthful Chong Ch'ol, educated him and arranged the marriage. His house was one of the great literary salons of the area.

[75] Ch'usok, the Harvest Moon Festival.

A Shijo Poet in the Court of King Sonjo

A razor wind sweeps up the leaves
   piled on bare mountain,
vexes the bundled clouds,
   drives the snow in front.
The Creator extravagantly
   makes jade flowers,
arrays in beauty
   a thousand grasses, ten thousand trees.
The shallows ahead are frozen;
   the single log bridge tilted.
To what temple
   is the old monk heading, staff in hand?
The aged mountain man
   does not wish to show these riches to others
lest outsiders come to the lovely jade cave
   of his secluded world.

No friend in these mountains;
   piles of yellow books;
through the ages
   with the men of old;
so many sages,
   so many heroes.
I suppose
   when heaven was created
the Creator ordained all things
   without a second thought.
Yet how could he devise the fortunes of any one time
   so full of ups and downs?
So many imponderables,
   so many things sad beyond compare.

Songgang kasa: The Pine River Songs

Why did the old sage of Mount Ji
   wash his ears?[76]
Throwing away the gourd
   enhanced his integrity.[77]

A man's nature is like his face:
   new every time you look.
The affairs of the world
   are threatening clouds.
I wonder how the wine we made some days ago
   has come on.
Take a cup, offer a cup,
   drink our fill;
the tribulations that knot the heart
   ease a little.
I pluck the strings of the *komun'go*;
   play "Wind in the Pines",
forget who is guest
   and who is master.

The crane flying in the sky
   is the Immortal of this valley.
By any chance have you seen it
   under Quartz Terrace in the moonlight?
Says guest to master:
   you're the Immortal here.

---

[76] The king asked Xu You, his most honest retainer, to accept the kingdom. Horrified, Xu You washed his ears and fled. He lived in seclusion on Mount Ji.

[77] Someone gave Xu You a gourd to drink water. Xu You threw it away because it made too much noise hanging in the wind.

Bibliography

Ch'oe T'aeho, *Chong Ch'ol munhangnon ko*, (Study of the literary works of Chong Ch'ol). Seoul: Toso ch'ulp'an yongnak, 2000.

Cho Tongil, "Kasaui changnu kyujong" (Defining the kasa genre), Omunhak 21 ho (1969), p. 85.

Cho, Kyuik, *Kagokch'angsaui kungmunhakchok ponjil* (The essence of the *kagok-ch'ang* song lyric in the Korean literature tradition). Seoul: Chimmundang, 1994.

Chong Ch'ol, *Songgang kasa* (The pine river songs), edited by Chon Yongjin, Seoul: Hongshin munhwasa 1995.

Chong Pyong'uk, *Hanguk kojonui chaeinshik* (A reappraisal of classical Korean literature). (Seoul: Sasongshinso), 1979.

Chong, Pyong'uk, *Shijo munhak sajon* (Dictionary of shijo literature). Seoul: Shin'gu munwhasa, 1974.

Hoyt, James, *Soaring Phoenixes and Prancing Dragons*, Chimmoondang, 2000.

Kim, Hunggyu, *Understanding Korean Literature*, translated by Robert J. Fouser. New York: Sharpe, 1987.

Lee, Peter (translated and edited), *Pine River and Lone Peak*. Honolulu: Hawaii University Press, 1991.

O'Rourke, Kevin, *The Book of Korean Shijo*. Cambridge: Harvard, 2002.

O'Rourke, Kevin, *The Shijo Tradition*. Seoul: Jongeumsa, 1987.

O'Rourke, Kevin, *Tilting the Jar, Spilling the Moon*. Dublin: Dedalus, 1993.

Pak Yongju, *Chong Ch'ol P'yongjon* (A critical biography of Chong Ch'ol. Seoul: Chungang M&B, 1999.

Pak, Ulsu, *Hanguk shijo taesajon* (Comprehensive dictionary of Korean shijo). Seoul: Asea munhwasa, 1992..

Rutt, Richard, *The Bamboo Grove*. Berkeley: University of California Press, 1971.

Shim, Chaewan, *Yokdae shijo chonso* (Compendium of shijo through the ages). Seoul: Sejong munhwasa, 1972.

So, Wonpyon, *Han'guk kasaui munhakchok yon'gu* (A literary study of Korean kasa). (Seoul: Hyongsol ch'ulp'ansa, 1995).

Index of First Lines

A man turns aside from the road	56
A shadow is reflected in the water	49
A sudden shower	43
A tall Shilla pagoda	43
A wayfarer, lodged on Mount Star	82
After a ten-year interval I see again	41
Ah, nephew! Nothing to eat	58
As I move the goosefoot forward	47
Big brother, little brother	55
Butterflies hover in pairs where flowers blossom thick	50
Clouds shrouded	48
Crane, flying high	37
Don't play dice or chess	59
Don't waken babies from sweet sleep	46
Fishermen of the Chu River	54
Forty thousand boxes of bright jewels	46
Genuine jade, they said	53
Holding back a horse laugh	42
How are you managing the bereavements in your house?	58
Human life lasts a hundred years	35
Husband and wife are one body in two	56
Husband dead	52
I followed you into this world	62
I promised to return to rivers and lakes	54
I race through Kwanghwamun	31
I say it once again	34
I wish to dismember my body	35
I'll cut out my heart	36
I'll wash and rewash	44

Index of First Lines

I'm aware that I'm not	40
I'm fifty now, no longer young	45
I've been gone such a very long time	47
If an elder takes you by the wrist	57
If I lifted my wings	35
If you truly hoped to achieve something	34
In the world of men is there anything	58
It's full daylight now	59
Lady hasting on your way, I know your face	67
Let's drink a cup of wine; let's drink another!	61
Listen here	33
My carelessness	45
My father gave me birth	55
My old loves are still my loves	44
No moaning, please	42
Now that I'm keeper of the state guesthouse	39
Now that I'm keeper of the state guesthouse	39
Now that I'm keeper of the state guesthouse	39
Old-timer, burdened head and back	60
On Pongnaesan where my true love lives	32
Stock from boiled bitter greens	32
Pearly raindrops on green hills	50
People of Kangwon Province	31
Reclined in the bamboo grove	71
Shall I put my worries aside	45
Sleep bound birds fly home	51
Snow falling in the pine forest	49
Somehow or other	46
Somewhere on Namsan Mountain	44
Take all the misfortunes	48
Ten years I followed you	34
That zelkova planted on the terrace	37
The evening sun slants low	51
The falling paulownia leaves	47
The lad has gone to dig fernbrake	49
The relationship between king and people	55
The rise and fall of nations are myriad	36
The tree is diseased	40
Though you go without clothes yourself	59
Two stone Buddhas, naked and fasting	51
Village people, let's do what is right	57
We'll strain sour wine and drink	42
Were I brilliant	50

Index of First Names

What happens if you pull down	41
When did Liu Ling live?	32
When did the leaves come out	53
When I strike the great string of the komun'go	38
When I think of King Chang Sha's tutor	40
When my long feathers molt	38
When our droopy-eared horse	48
When Shin Kunmang was a fifth rank official	36
When the paulownia leaves fell	54
When the South Pole Star	37
Where has the crane gone	43
Where is that boat going	52
Whether I eat wheat bran or rice chaff	33
While your parents are alive	56
White gull	53
Why does that pine tree stand	52
Yesterday I heard that Master Song	41
Your son is reading the Book of Filial Piety	57

For Product Safety Concerns and Information please contact our EU representative GPSR@taylorandfrancis.com
Taylor & Francis Verlag GmbH, Kaufingerstraße 24, 80331 München, Germany